on track ...
Talking Heads

every album, every song

David Starkey

sonicbondpublishing.com

Sonicbond Publishing Limited
www.sonicbondpublishing.co.uk
Email: info@sonicbondpublishing.co.uk

First Published in the United Kingdom 2025
First Published in the United States 2025

British Library Cataloguing in Publication Data:
A Catalogue record for this book is available from the British Library

Copyright David Starkey 2025

ISBN 978-1-78952-353-9

The right of David Starkey to be identified
as the author of this work has been asserted by him
in accordance with the Copyright, Designs and Patents Act 1988.
All rights reserved. No part of this publication may be reproduced, stored in a
retrieval system or transmitted in any form or by any means, electronic, mechanical,
photocopying, recording or otherwise, without prior permission in writing from
Sonicbond Publishing Limited

Typeset in ITC Garamond Std & ITC Avant Garde Gothic
Printed and bound in England

Graphic design and typesetting: Full Moon Media

Follow us on social media:
Twitter: https://twitter.com/SonicbondP
Instagram: www.instagram.com/sonicbondpublishing_/
Facebook: www.facebook.com/SonicbondPublishing/

Linktree QR code:

For Sandy

I come home, she lifted up her wings
I guess that this must be the place

'This Must Be The Place (Naive Melody)'

Acknowledgements

Whenever possible, I turned to the members of Talking Heads for information about the composition and recording of their songs. Chris Frantz's *Remain In Love* (St. Martin's, 2020) and David Byrne's *How Music Works* (McSweeney's, 2012) were both invaluable. *Talking Heads: The Band And Their Music* (Avon, 1985) by David Gans is long out of print, but it remains a rich source of commentary by band members about their work up to *Little Creatures*. Ian Gittins' *Talking Heads: Once In A Lifetime: The Stories Behind Every Song* (Hal Leonard, 2004) was a helpful precursor to my own book. Probably the best overall coverage of the band is offered by David Bowman's *This Must Be The Place: The Adventures Of Talking Heads In The 20th Century* (Harper Entertainment, 2001.) (The book's original title *Fa Fa Fa Fa Fa Fa* is a hoot, alluding as it does to the chorus of 'Psycho Killer'.) Jonathan Lethem's *Fear Of Music* – an entry in Bloomsbury's 33 1/3 series, delves deeply into that album.

Outside the realm of traditional print sources, Rodney Gordon's podcast *This Must Be Talking Heads* – an album-by-album look at the band – was a great boon to someone writing an *On Track* book about Talking Heads: it's also a lot of fun. In addition, I benefited from various online band-member interviews, which are cited in-text, and especially from the *Rolling Stone* and Robert Christgau reviews of each album, which were always insightful and well-written. When I needed to find that last little bit of information about a song, I often relied on the website discogs. com, which includes images of album and CD covers, record sleeves, booklets, liner notes, track information, etc.

Many thanks, of course, to Stephen Lambe and the Sonicbond team for including this essential band in their *On Track* series.

Finally, I want to give a special shout-out to my friend David Sherman, a true Talking Heads fanatic. Prior to and during the writing of this book, David was more than willing to bounce around ideas, argue for or against a particular interpretation of a song, help me track down an obscure source, and generally keep me aware of just how special a band Talking Heads was, is, and always will be.

on track ...
Talking Heads

Contents

Introduction: My Friends Are Important............9
Talking Heads: 77 (1977)...............15
More Songs About Buildings And Food (1978)............25
Fear Of Music (1979)............34
Remain In Light (1980)............45
The Name Of This Band Is Talking Heads (Live) (1982)............56
Speaking In Tongues (1983)............63
Stop Making Sense (Live) (1984)............74
Little Creatures (1985)............80
True Stories (1986)............90
Naked (1988)............100
Studio Songs Not Included On The Original Studio Albums............113
Epilogue............121

Introduction: My Friends Are Important

Rock and roll has always allowed – even encouraged – people to lean into their idiosyncrasies. Think of the gender-busting personae of Little Richard and hillbilly madman Jerry Lee Lewis, or for that matter, nerdy Buddy Holly in his huge horn-rim glasses. Even Elvis Presley was considered slightly crazy before he became cool.

The four members of Talking Heads – lead singer and guitarist David Byrne, drummer Chris Frantz, bassist Tina Weymouth and guitarist and keyboardist Jerry Harrison – came of age as a band during the heady punk-rock years of the late 1970s: an era that was particularly welcoming to misfits.

In 1975, beginning as a trio (minus Harrison), the band began playing at New York's punk haven on the Bowery, CBGB (which inaccurately stood for 'Country, Bluegrass, Blues'), home of Patti Smith, Television, Blondie, The Misfits, The Dead Boys, The Cramps and a host of others. The biggest of all in that initially very small scene were The Ramones. Their look and attitude helped define punk – nearly braindead goons in leather jackets; they played as though speed was perpetually running through their veins. They sang about pinheads, chainsaw massacres, sniffing glue and selling sex on 53rd and 3rd. They were – to borrow the title of the first Dead Boys album – young, loud and snotty.

Talking Heads went the opposite route. They were far more Buddy Holly than Little Richard or Elvis, and they looked like the nerdy college kids they were. However, their nerdy lead singer didn't sing about frat parties or final exams. He crooned about being a misfit, particularly in the realm of love. Although CBGB owner Hilly Kristal wrote on the club's retrospective website that Byrne 'had a voice like a wavering scarecrow', the band was welcomed into the fold, in part because – as Chris Frantz reported in his memoir *Remain In Love* – Johnny Ramone, the guitarist, said, 'Yeah, they suck, so they can open for us. They'll make us look good'.

In a 1983 *Rolling Stone* interview with Christopher Connelly, Byrne recalled Talking Heads' early shows at CBGB: 'There might have been 20 people in there, but they really seemed to appreciate what we were doing'. However, he also acknowledged that his stage persona could be off-putting: 'I've seen some of the early shows on videotape, and they are a little disturbing. But there was still some humor there. I did understand that the performances were a little odd and that people carried that over and thought I was a little odd. But I thought it was a failing of mine that I wasn't clear enough, that some parts were meant to be funny'.

In 1977, with a record contract on the horizon, the original three members talked the more experienced Jerry Harrison into joining the group. Unlike most punk groups, who began playing shows the moment they had even half an idea for a song (I must admit that my own band, The Assholes, fell into that category in the late-1970s), Talking Heads practiced for six months before taking the stage at CBGB. Awkward and geeky though they may have been, they believed in their material and they knew how to play it, and Harrison recognized that he would be joining a potentially successful band

But who were these four individuals who in 2002 would be inducted into the Rock and Roll Hall of Fame? Surely, they each had a remarkable background to account for the synergy that resulted in their combined musical efforts. Well, yes and no.

The Band
David Byrne

David Byrne, the guitarist, lead singer and main songwriter for Talking Heads, was born in Dumbarton, Scotland (a town just northwest of Glasgow) in 1952, though his family (he has one sister, Emma) moved to Hamilton, Ontario, when Byrne was just two. When he was seven, they moved again, this time to suburban Baltimore, where his father took a job as an engineer for Westinghouse.

In his book *How Music Works*, Byrne says that, as a teenager, he was 'incredibly shy... a withdrawn introvert'. On Talking Heads' official website, he recounts his early musical experiences as follows: 'Went to public school, was respectfully kicked out of the choir and given lots of encouragement by the high school art teacher. Had violin lessons, but the teacher was mean and I was terrible. Taught myself guitar and ukulele and played rock songs at local coffee houses and folk clubs'. The encouragement from his art teacher was one reason why, in 1970, he enrolled in the prestigious Rhode Island School of Design (RISD), though he dropped out after a year. Eventually, Byrne returned to Providence, where he teamed up with old friend Chris Frantz, and the two of them began playing together as The Artistics (a band name that surely had a resonance for Byrne, who later came to believe he was autistic.) According to Frantz in *Remain In Love*, the band 'only played four shows', but each one was an event: 'When The Artistics began to play, people came running. The smell of marijuana was in the air, and the mood was colorful, festive and celebratory': not exactly the description of an early Talking Heads concert.

In the summer of 1974, Byrne moved to New York with Frantz; Frantz's girlfriend Martina (as she was then known) Weymouth followed later that fall. Soon, the three began rehearsing in earnest, and in May 1975, they played their first gig at CBGB.

Chris Frantz

Chris Frantz was born in Fort Campbell, Kentucky, in 1951. His father had a successful career in the military, so Frantz, even more than Byrne, had a peripatetic childhood. However, Frantz's recollection of his family situation is considerably sunnier than Byrne's. In *Remain In Love*, Frantz describes his father as 'a tall, good-looking, bright, young army officer ... and my mother was a real knockout, a Southern belle'. Frantz adapted well to the different places his family moved, living, by most accounts, a fairly healthy and normal childhood. He especially loved visiting his grandparents in Mason County, Kentucky, where he describes his summers as 'wonderfully free'. Like Byrne, Frantz showed an early interest in art and music. After an unsuccessful stint on the trumpet, he began playing drums in local rock bands and, like Byrne, he was accepted at RISD in 1970. However, unlike Byrne, Frantz finished his degree, graduating in 1974. As noted above, Frantz moved with his girlfriend Tina to New York, where they rented 'a raw loft at 195 Christie Street', and the focus of their lives soon became the band Talking Heads.

Tina Weymouth

Martina 'Tina' Weymouth was also born to a military family. The third of eight children, she began life in 1950 at Naval Air Station, Coronado, California, but lived all over the world. 'Moving every year or so', she writes on the band's website, 'we crisscrossed the country and two oceans on various tours of duty, including Hawaii, France and Iceland. To grow up in a family that loved the service and travel was a great experience'.

Like Byrne and Frantz, Weymouth had an early love for art and music, taking drawing lessons at the Corcoran School of Art and learning folk songs on the acoustic guitar. Weymouth spent her first two years in college at Barnard, studying art history and French literature. (She's fluent in the language, which is her mother's native tongue.) For her final two years as an undergraduate, she transferred to RISD, where she devoted herself full-time to making art and shared a painting studio with Frantz. After the move to New York, when no one else seemed to want to join Byrne and Frantz as their bass player, Weymouth used the birthday money her parents sent her and bought a bass guitar, becoming an essential member of Talking Heads. 'As we shared a sensibility', she noted, 'Chris's idea was that it would be easier for me to pick up the bass to be molded by them than for another to understand what he and David were going after'.

Jerry Harrison

The oldest Talking Head, born in 1949 in Milwaukee, Harrison was also the only member of the group to have experience as a professional musician prior to the formation of the band. Unlike the other members, he spent his childhood in his hometown, where both his parents were involved in the arts, though his father was also an executive at an advertising firm. Like Frantz, Harrison was an active member of local rock bands. He graduated from Harvard, Magna Cum Laude, in 1972 in the field of Visual and Environmental Studies, and later that year met Jonathan Richman. They formed the Modern Lovers with Harrison on keyboards and background vocals, recording their self-titled debut album in 1972. Though it is now considered a proto-punk classic, the record was not distributed until 1976, long after the band had broken up due to artistic differences and Harrison had returned to Harvard to study architecture. In 1976, he received a phone call from Weymouth asking him to leave Boston for New York to play with the band. Harrison was initially reluctant, but after the release of Talking Heads' debut single 'Love → Building On Fire', he was convinced, and he joined in 1977 in time for the recording of their first album.

In his autobiography *Remain In Love*, Frantz recounts how the band got their name: 'We tried The Vogue Dots, The Billionaires, The Tunnel Tones, The Videos, but none of them stuck'. Then their friend Wayne Zieve (who wrote the lyric to 'Artists Only' on the second Talking Heads album, *More Songs About Buildings And Food*) told them he'd been flipping through a *TV Guide*. Zieve said: 'When you have a shot of just the announcer's head and shoulders, it's called a Talking Head. It's the most boring but also the most informative format on TV. I think you should call your band Talking Heads'. All agreed it was 'a brilliant name that did not connote any particular style of music'.

Nevertheless, early Talking Heads *did* play a particular style of music. It's been variously described as brittle, edgy, spasmodic, agitated, angular, cryptic, weird, funky, danceable, and a host of other adjectives, many of which ring true, but none of which on their own truly capture the magic of the band's sound. Hilly Kristal said they sounded like 'a metronome gone awry', but that doesn't give credit to Byrne's wickedly good rhythm guitar-playing, Frantz's impeccable timing, Weymouth's minimalist-genius bass lines or Harrison's flawless sense of when to add an instrument and when to drop-out.

'Musically… and visually, we felt very, very different than what was then considered punk rock', Byrne said in a 2023 interview with Terry Gross on *Fresh Air*, 'but we had this kind of DIY: the do-it-yourself idea that was prevalent amongst the punk rockers … and we could speak to the concerns of our generation and our contemporaries'. Of course, that's not to say that Talking Heads' sound was completely *sui generis*. The Velvet Underground are a clear – if sometimes refracted – influence and the jangly guitars of Television (whose album *Marquee Moon* was released in February 1977) ring familiar bells. Another sonic cousin of the band's debut album, *Talking Heads: 77,* is *Blank Generation* by their Sire labelmates Richard Hell and the Voidoids. The two albums were released in the same month, but all these sounds were in the air in 1976 and 1977, with groups attending each other's gigs and listening to, learning from, copying, extending and betraying the sounds of their peers.

It's also worth repeating that Talking Heads' *look* – so different from the standard punk outfit of black t-shirts and torn blue jeans – often made just as much an impression on concertgoers as the music. In *This Must Be The Place: The Adventures Of Talking Heads In The 20th Century*, David Bowman describes photographs of the early band at a private party in a New Jersey living room with 'awful orange' carpet, 'ruffled curtains' and three ceramic fish hanging on the wall (see the cover of *The Name Of This Band Is Talking Heads*):

There's something incongruous about the whole event, these four peculiar musicians, Satan (Harrison), Norman Bates (Byrne), Jean Seberg (Weymouth) … and the happy-go-lucky Ringo (Frantz) playing ascetic electric funk with cybernetic lyrics about having 'no compassion' on this 'happy day' in the heart of suburbia.

And yet, that apparent mishmash of personal styles melded seamlessly into the music they created. Talking Heads caught the interest of so many people because they were so *different* from every other group on the scene.

A great deal – especially early on – was made of Byrne's voice, which, though it sounded nothing at all like Bob Dylan's, seemed just as revolutionary to listeners of the time. Byrne sang in tune, but his voice was high-pitched, sometimes shrill, with a deadpan effect that was periodically upended when he would burst into a shouted run of nonsense syllables. In a hilarious self-interview appended to the DVD of *Stop Making Sense*, Byrne, dressed as a cantankerous old man, says, 'I don't think you have a very good voice. But you're a singer. How do you do that?' Dressed in his famous big suit, Byrne replies, 'The better a singer's voice, the harder it is to believe what they're saying, so I use my faults to an advantage'. Indeed, the most distinctive element of Talking Heads was always Byrne's voice. Frantz pays grudging respect to Byrne's vocal talents in *Remain In Love*:

David was not anybody's idea of a good singer, but he was our idea of a great vocalist. He sang with real feeling, and in his weird vocal style, you could hear the pain of creation. His style was personal and was not riding on the coattails of any other singer. He sounded heartfelt and could also be very amusing.

Just as striking as the band's music, if not more so, were Byrne's lyrics. In David Gans' essential collection of the group's commentary on their own work *Talking Heads: The Band And Their Music* (hereafter referred to as *The Band And Their Music*), Weymouth offers an insight into Byrne's personality that indirectly explains the content of many of his lyrics:

He was always afraid of becoming an ordinary person. And I think he wanted to be unique and individual, so he would do sort of whacked-out things instead of slipping into the mainstream, which is kind of painful for a shy person – sort of brave and a little bit crazy, too.

Reflecting on Byrne's early songwriting, Chris Connelly wrote in *Rolling Stone*:

Unlike the lit-drenched, punch-drunk verbiage of Dylan or Springsteen, Byrne's lyrics were as terse as mathematical formulas. He took cultural clichés – on everything from true love to civic pride – out of their customary contexts and stitched them instead into Pinter-esque pastiches, whose odd juxtapositions and things left unspoken were rich with wit and insight.

Talking Heads aficionados spend a great amount of time trying to figure out just what David Byrne's lyrics mean, and I'll inevitably be doing quite a bit of that myself, despite the fact that he has stated on countless occasions that he comes up with the words in a slow process that favors sound over meaning. For instance, in a 2010 interview with John Sutter of CNN, Byrne reiterated that song lyrics are overrated: 'People ignore them half the time. In a certain way, it's the sound of the words, the inflection, the way the song is sung, the way it fits the melody and the way the syllables are on the tongue – that has as much of the meaning as the actual, literal words'. As Rodney Gordon of the essential podcast *This Must Be Talking Heads* put it: 'Many of David's lyrics are what we call non-sequiturs. They don't really make sense, but they sound great'.

Regardless of any reservations people might have had about Talking Heads, after a year of playing at CBGB and other local clubs, they were undeniably hot and part of a scene where just about everyone was getting a record deal. In November 1976, after recording several demos for CBS that the company rejected, the band signed with Seymour Stein's Sire Records, and a few months later, they began recording their first album.

Talking Heads: 77 (1977)

Personnel:
David Byrne: guitar, lead vocals
Chris Frantz: drums, steel pan
Jerry Harrison: guitar, keyboards, backing vocals
Tina Weymouth (credited as Martina Weymouth): bass
Producers: Tony Bongiovi, Lance Quinn, Talking Heads
Recorded: January-April, June 1977
Studio: Sundragon, New York City
Release date: 16 September 1977
Running time: 38:37
Label: Sire
Album charts: US: 97, UK: 60
Singles charts: 'Psycho Killer', US: 92

By early 1977, Talking Heads had more than enough first-rate material for an album, and their constant gigging meant they had the songs down cold. Making the record should have been an easy process. The band was hoping to work with former Velvet Underground member John Cale as producer, but he was considered insufficiently 'commercial' by Seymour Stein. Instead, the group entered the now defunct Sundragon Studio on West 20th Street with Tony Bongiovi (Jon Bon Jovi's second cousin), which resulted in what Byrne called in *How Music Works*, 'by and large a miserable experience. Nothing really sounded like it did in our heads or like we were used to hearing ourselves on stage'. Byrne says while the group admired Bongiovi's production of several disco hits, they felt that he 'didn't 'get' what we were about'.

In *Remain In Love*, Frantz further describes the less-than-satisfactory relationship the band had with Bongiovi: 'Tony asked us to do six or eight tracks of each song, far beyond the point where a great take had already been recorded ... We felt Tony was condescending to the band, reading magazines about airplanes while we worked. He was repeatedly rude to Tina. Let's just say he appeared clueless and was not a gentleman'. Bongiovi was determined to have a hit, and he didn't care how the band felt about his methods of getting there. As a result of their poor relationship with him, the band began to record when Bongiovi was out of the studio. They worked much better with co-producer Lance Quinn and engineer Ed Stasium, finishing 'the basic tracks, guide vocals and a few guitar and keyboard overdubs in less than two weeks'.

At that point – spring 1977 – they were given the opportunity to open for The Ramones on a European tour, and they jumped at the opportunity. It was apparently a formative experience: Frantz spends more than 40 pages of his book on those few months. After the tour, feeling confident and worldly, they completed the final overdubs in New York, and the album was released in September.

The front cover, based on an idea by Byrne, is mostly day-glo orange, with the title at the top in a vibrant, practically vibrating green. The back cover photograph by Mick Rock is shot from above and shows the band looking, well, very *average* for a group of musicians. Their hair is well-coiffed, their clothes unspectacular. For instance, Byrne is wearing a plaid shirt. For a group who cut its teeth in the grime and noise of CBGB, they don't look very threatening. Nevertheless, *Talking Heads: 77* is a very punk album. Transform Harrison's synthesizer into a Farfisa organ and turn the distortion way up on those trebly guitars, and the impact of their formative *milieu* would be obvious. But even in its actual incarnation, the record reflects punk's energy: some of it jubilant, some of it nihilistic.

In *Talking Heads: Once In A Lifetime* (hereafter referred to as *Once In A Lifetime*), Ian Gittins describes the album as a 'minor masterpiece'. He calls it 'minimalist yet complex, cerebral yet visceral, rudimentary and yet undoubtedly progressive. This was thoroughly modern music, lush with textural possibilities and pregnant with the anxieties of urban dwelling. Forget any notions of arid, art-school rock: these urgent songs were coming equally from both the cranium and the loins'. Gittins is far from alone in his appreciation of the album. Writing in the *New York Post* in 1977, Carl Arrington noted, 'Their lyrics are full of deceptively banal subjects ... but are clever, and remind the reviewer of the type of pop lyrics Samuel Beckett might write if given the chance. They have been called 'minimalists', which, translated, means they write and perform without wasting musical space'.

Things were going well for Talking Heads. Frantz and Weymouth were married in June 1977, and the album was released on 16 September. *Talking Heads: 77* placed seventh in *The Village Voice*'s annual Pazz & Jop poll of best albums. In his review in the *Voice*, Robert Christgau pointed out that 'In the end, the record proves not only that the detachment of craft can co-exist with a frightening intensity of feeling – something most artists know – but that the most inarticulate rage can be rationalized'. Indeed, that would be a hallmark of Byrne's performances with the band: a weird detachment coupled with an equally weird intensity.

'Parsing the blend of sincerity and irony in any Talking Heads song is difficult', wrote Andy Cush in a retrospective review of the album on the website *Pitchfork*, 'but you never doubt their belief in the music'. Indeed, whatever one thinks of *Talking Heads: 77*, its energy and passion are palpable, and it deserves the enduring place it has found in lists like *Rolling Stone's 500 Greatest Albums Of All Time* and *1001 Albums You Must Hear Before You Die*.

'Uh-Oh, Love Comes To Town' (Byrne)
Right from the beginning, Talking Heads were an *unusual* band. Granted, the album's opening track begins with Weymouth's funky bass riff, which could have been the engine of many a pop song of the late-1970s. It's pleasant and

danceable until the singer interrupts. A white male tenor, he seems to be reaching for the highest notes in his range. 'Love is simple as 1-2-3', he says in the concluding line of the opening verse, apparently alluding to the Jackson Five's 'ABC', although he doesn't sound much like Michael Jackson or someone given to simplicity. Then Byrne veers from the standard love song *cliché*, telling his beloved that he's the 'smartest man around', with Harrison's menacing synthesizer note beneath the singing. A lovely and unexpected steel drum break played by Frantz seems to tug the song back toward the world of normality. However, the singer has other ideas. He has 'called in sick' to be with his sweetheart, 'the smartest girl in town'. Indeed, he plans to neglect his duties and get in trouble, but that's okay because he's 'been to college/been to school/met the people that you read about in books'.' *Dude*', you can imagine his paramour saying to the singer. *Whoa.*

Then a horn section (uncredited in the liner notes) comes up behind the chorus, emphasizing the three unlikely descriptions we are about to hear, suggesting that the singer is like a 'jet pilot gone out of control', a 'ship Captain on the ground' or a stockbroker who has made a bad investment. Less than two minutes into the first song on their first album, and how far we have come from the opening invitation for the singer's girl to take his hand and 'believe in mystery'.

Back come the steel drums, adding grace notes to the singer's admission that he has lost his common sense and is in 'a jam like this'. All the while, the bass is following its predictable, syncopated pattern, though the horns on the final chorus are practically bursting through the mix as Byrne almost screams the final obvious answer to why he is behaving so erratically: 'Love has come to town'.

'New Feeling' (Byrne)
Seven seconds into a funky lead guitar introduction, 'New Feeling' devolves into two trebly, off-kilter guitars playing against each other, one in each speaker, creating a sound that is not entirely pleasant. As in the opening number, the bass is upfront, accompanied by Frantz's confident drumming. In a 2020 interview with *Slate*'s Kurt Andersen, Byrne described the song as 'a little bit funky, but kind of stiff sounding, but to me it successfully didn't quite sound like much else'. That's certainly true. The opening verse lyric depicts the singer struggling with self-control and paradox. He goes visiting and he talks loudly. He tries to make himself clear, presumably without success. Then he's in front of a face that is 'Nearer than it's ever been before'; 'not this close before', he repeats nervously. Uh-oh, a listener might think, what's going on?

After the first verse, the opening guitar riff returns with its brief nod to normalcy before the off-balance second verse. (Apropos of its title, there's no real chorus in 'New Feeling'.) Now, the singer is claiming not only that 'It is a million years ago', but also that he hears music in his head which 'sounds like bells'. He screeches a bit when singing the word 'music', as though it's something greater than himself or something he doesn't entirely trust or understand. Without any evident transition, he tells us that he wants to 'meet everyone' and bring them up to his room. One can picture that room as a small place, probably dark, capable of hosting a few guests at most – hardly an abode that can accommodate 'everyone'.

Following another revisiting of the guitar riff, the singer is 'busy again', though he feels like sitting down, and again, there's a bit of yelp to go with 'sitting down', as if he didn't really want to do it. But soon, rather than sitting or being otherwise occupied, he's 'Speaking out/Speaking about my friends'. What friends, of course, one wonders, does this lonely oddball actually have? Are they imaginary? Or, like the psycho killer we will meet in the album's penultimate track, does he have other plans? Are these folks that the singer plans to kill and inter in his lonely room?

In the outro, the guitar riff has lost its bounce. It sounds almost menacing, and Byrne, elongating the word 'frie-eh-ends', slips into a wordless semi-scream with the song ending abruptly. Whatever this singer's new feeling is meant to evoke, it is hardly one of placidity and resolve.

'Tentative Decisions' (Byrne)

This track opens with the sort of afro rhythm that was to later reappear on *Fear Of Music*. Byrne enters quickly, singing – in a kind of robotic voice – that he wants to release his tensions and make clear his 'best intentions'. Meanwhile, he's fielding odd queries from girls ('Can I define decision?') and boys ('Can I describe their function?'). It's an unusual prelude to the rest of the song, which suddenly becomes much grander, with Frantz's military drumming accompanying Byrne's triple-tracked vocal that continues his disquisition on the difference between boys and girls. Boys want to talk about their problems, while girls are 'concerned with decisiveness' – a clever reversal of conventional gender expectations. Harrison accentuates the simple melody on acoustic piano, which contrasts nicely with Frantz's busy drumming.

In the next verse, a growling, lower-pitched Byrne speaks the first three words of the lines that the tenor-voiced Byrne will then sing: 'I wanna talk as much as I want/I wanna give the problem to you'. The two lines are repeated, and it's now clear by the album's third song that the protagonist of these songs is someone having a hard time figuring out his place in the world.

Indeed, 'Who the hell is this person?' we may be wondering by the following verse when he seems to be issuing orders. But to whom? The boys? The girls? Himself? (It doesn't seem unlikely that he has multiple personalities.) Or is he speaking to the possibly invented 'friends' from the previous song? 'Decide, decide', he sings, but then it's 'Confuse, confuse'. Perhaps these are the tentative decisions of the song's title. But as the brisk drumming gets louder, it's hard to know just what we are supposed to be thinking, which is perhaps the point.

The afro rhythm of the opening bars is reprised, with a few notes of bass solo for good measure, then the entire prior structure, minus the opening verse, repeats. But this time, it's the girls who want to talk about problems and the boys who are concerned with decisiveness. If the lyrics are just as enigmatic as they were the first time around, repetition makes them feel more familiar. So even if we aren't sure what's going on, we have the illusion that maybe we are starting to figure things out.

The final half minute is a piano-led coda with a long fadeout. As the music retreats to silence, a listener may be wondering, 'What did I just hear?' – a question equally relevant after the first or 50th encounter with this song.

'Happy Day' (Byrne)

'Happy Day' begins appropriately with a happy, almost mellow vibe, with guitars going back and forth from one channel to the other. We're suspicious by now that a pleasant-sounding introduction won't stick around for long in a Talking Heads song, but the music stays relatively upbeat. Even when minor chords are introduced into the verse, the effect is piquant rather than morose. The lyric – not surprisingly – is another matter. The singer seems uncertain about how to proceed with his sensations: 'I want to talk …/Before I decide what to do'. In the pre-chorus, which bounces between major and minor chords, the singer falls over and can't stand up; he can't be critical and his 'heart won't stop'. It's hardly the sort of rush of affirmation one expects to precede a four-line chorus that uses 'Happy day' four times, but the chorus feels only tangentially happy. Indeed, 'day' is sung in an even higher register as 'day-a-a', as though it would be wrong somehow not to give it an ironic twist. In fact, each time the chorus recurs (two more times), that single happy day on which the speaker is fixated begins to feel more distant, perhaps imaginary, and certainly not happy in the way most pop songs would define the word. And yet, if this is the happiest our singer can feel, there is perhaps something innocent and sweet hiding beneath the admission that this is 'The story I told/The story I made up'. In the third and final verse – where the singer feels 'some density' moving beside him before he announces, 'I want my sentence right here/But now I'm far away' – the disturbing images feel like …

All the way through, Weymouth's cheery bass provides a familiar, sometimes winking commentary on the proceedings. Fittingly, in the interlude after the first two choruses, a perky guitar figure accompanied by Harrison's bell-like synthesizer sound seems to want to draw us back into a world of romance, no matter how impossible that may be for the singer to achieve.

'Who Is It?' (Byrne)

The fifth song begins with in-your-face funk: both guitars, bass and drums all working together to create a slightly weird but danceable groove. At less than two minutes, the song is something of a one-trick pony, without any of the lyrical complexity of the previous tracks. Byrne explained decades later on the *This Must Be Talking Heads* podcast: 'I wanted to write a love song as direct as I could be, and eliminate sort of all the metaphors and things, like, you know, your love is like a pomegranate'. In fact, he has eliminated everything but a handful of words. The verses consist of Byrne asking four times, 'Who, who is it?' and 'What is it?' The answer, in the classic pop-song vernacular, is 'Baby, it's you'. Because of the lyrical monotony, the band needs to carry the song, and they do it with unrestrained energy.

The bridge does return to some of the semi-sinister wordplay of the previous songs, as the singer warns the person he has his eye on: 'Watch out now, Baby/'Cause I'm in love with you'. Should she feel uncomfortable with that declaration, he has a response: 'If you don't love me/I don't know what I'm going to do'. Something inappropriate, one supposes.

But as the song returns to its groove, with 'Who, who, who is it?' stated eight times now, a closer comparison might be to Talking Heads' CBGB compatriots The Ramones, who used repetition to sublime effect.

'No Compassion' (Byrne)

If the singer has seemed strange and often overbearing on previous tracks, here he is positively boorish. Presumably, this is a stage persona Byrne has adopted. But what makes it so unsettling is that he never cracks a smile. A listener might wonder how close the singer is to the actual man. (In *Remain In Love*, Frantz wrote, 'With what we now know', Byrne was on the 'high-functioning end of the spectrum ... When you played music with David, you came to realize that his eccentricities were not an act'.)

'No Compassion' has a big opening, with the guitars fuller than in other songs and the bass and drums up front. After several repetitions of the four-chord pattern, Byrne plays a slide-guitar part that is anything but bluesy. The singing is matter-of-fact, with the end rhymes imperfect and the lyrics themselves sounding more like prose than poetry. The first verse is languid, ending with the unsympathetic statement, 'They say compassion is a virtue/ But I don't have much time'.

One minute in, the song slows almost to a stop, then increases in tempo. A listener might think a new song had begun if not for the singer's continuing lack of empathy for other people's difficulties: 'So many people have their problems/I'm not interested in their problems'. He practically shouts how little he cares: 'My interest level is dropping/I've heard all I want to/And I don't want to hear any more'. On and on, he continues with his lack of compassion: 'Go talk to your analyst/Isn't that what they're paid for?'

At 3:15, the song comes to a false ending before the intro chords return, with the slide guitar now even more eerie and off-kilter. The first verse repeats, then the song seems to be coming to a close when Byrne announces 'Here we go again', and the second faster part comes back for a few more bars of outro. The overall vibe is both unsettling and catchy – classic Talking Heads.

'The Book I Read' (Byrne)

When *Talking Heads: 77* was released, listeners typically had two methods of listening to it: vinyl albums and cassette tapes. Turning the record or tape over signaled that one section had come to an end, and a new one was about to begin, with the first song on side two as important as the first line of a two-verse poem. 'The Book I Read' would, therefore, have been listened to with extra attention, and it deserves its important spot on the album.

The song begins with an intricate single-string guitar figure that leads to what initially sounds like the most romantic lyric on the album so far. Not only has the object of the singer's affection 'touched a soft spot' in his heart but it turns out that the book he's read was written by her. In verse two, we learn that the book is only a metaphor, and what the singer read was actually in her eyes. By verse three, he is feeling wonderful, 'tipping over backwards', and in verse four, he is 'spinning around but all right'. Harrison's piano and organ add to the lush sound, and when Byrne first sings 'Na na na na', the song practically has the feel of a top-40 hit.

However, when we listen closer to verse three, we realize the tropes may not be so comforting. Weirdly, the singer is 'so ambitious' and he's 'running a race' and she (the entire person now, we've been told, not just her eyes) is the book he read. It hardly sounds like *Love Story*, even less so when he begins singing 'Na na na na' yet again. At first these nonsense syllables – underpinned by bass and Harrison's piano and then organ – might be heard as utterances of joy and adoration. But they keep going on and on: the lover doesn't know when to stop announcing his love. As his singing becomes more out of control and even aggressive, Byrne accentuates the frenetic mood with rapid guitar strokes. By the end, the meaningless vocalizing feels like the heart and soul of the track, with the lover's eyes a distant memory.

'Don't Worry About The Government' (Byrne)

While 'Psycho Killer' is the album's most famous track, 'Don't Worry About the Government' is perhaps its most ambitious. Atypically for *Talking Heads: 77*, the singer begins by observing the beauty of the natural world. He sees 'The clouds that move across the sky' and 'The pine cones that fall by the highway', and he smells 'The pine trees and the peaches in the woods'. 'Bucolic' is hardly a word one associates with early Talking Heads, but there it is in the first two verses.

Nevertheless, it's not long before we can't help but feel that a heavy dollop of irony is being served up by a band that cut its teeth at CBGBs. The singer tells us how much he loves the building he lives in and how he wants his 'loved ones' and friends to come visit him. It's an odd sentiment that just gets odder in the song's second half when we learn that the singer has favorite laws and he believes, 'Some civil servants are just like my loved ones/They work so hard and they try to be strong'. 'Yeah, right', the street kid waiting online for a show in the Bowery might well think, and that irony feels hammered home by the steady bass and drums, as though the rhythm section couldn't generate enough enthusiasm to come up with something more interesting.

However, Ian Gittins reported that Weymouth said much later that the song was 'just us saying that the best rock 'n' roll comes out of the suburbs. It was a beautiful and innocent sentiment'. In a 2019 interview in *Vulture*, Byrne reiterated that notion: 'Everybody thought I was being ironic with the song because of the lyrics and the context. But I think people will see a certain truth to it now. It's not a great virtue to live in an apartment filled with cockroaches. You don't have to have a penthouse, but people want to have a decent life'.

Appropriately for a song claiming a kind of countrified sincerity, mandolin-like guitars open the track, with the singer quickly jumping to assert his love for modern conveniences. When he sings, 'My building has every convenience/It's gonna make life easy for me', the music rises up with acoustic guitars ringing out against the emphatic bass and drums. But how can we not hear the singer's plea – *four times* – that people shouldn't worry about him as anything but a call for help? Who else but someone deeply distressed would be so insistent on his own well-being? Indeed, at the very end, Byrne holds the final word in the phrase 'Don't you worry 'bout *meeee*' as though his life practically depended on it.

Interestingly, a similar naive everyman persona was to reappear nine years later on the *True Stories* cut 'People Like Us', where the singer positively declares that those of his ilk don't want freedom or justice; they just 'want someone to love'. Indeed.

'First Week/Last Week... Carefree' (Byrne)

The music on *Talking Heads: 77* is fairly uniform, but there are hints of the global experiments in sound that would come later. One of those moments takes place at the beginning of this track when the guiro (a Latin American percussion instrument) provides a striking rhythmic accompaniment to one of the collection's most impenetrable lyrics.

In an album full of bizarre narrators, the persona here is among the strangest. In the book *This Must Be The Place*, David Bowman describes the ambiance in 'First Week/Last Week... Carefree' as 'a kind of fake innocence skewed with Mediterranean beach vibe ... Gidget cast as one of the characters in F. Scott Fitzgerald's *Tender Is The Night*'. That might be stretching things, for the song's setting is unclear. Nevertheless, I imagine a surreal office environment. Is the singer a demented dentist? A deranged psychiatrist? Or is he an office temp, one whose first week and last week of employment are the same? Women's voices, incomplete reports, rescheduled appointments – whatever is happening here, it isn't business as usual.

Despite the lyrical confusion, the music remains upbeat throughout, and the (again uncredited) horns that show up for the breaks could have come directly from the Stax Records catalog or Talking Heads' first single, 'Love → Building

On Fire'. A marimba adds to the party atmosphere, though Byrne's periodic 'Ay ay ay's don't exactly work for a fiesta, sounding anything but carefree.

'Psycho Killer' (Byrne, Frantz, Weymouth)

This was Talking Heads' first song resembling a hit, and it remains one of their most recognizable and popular. By the time we arrive at the album's tenth song, after so many permutations of the unreliable narrator, we have little trouble imagining the singer as a psycho killer. Byrne spoke to Terry Gross on her radio show *Fresh Air*:

> I thought I would try and write something that was maybe a cross between Alice Cooper and Randy Newman ... I thought I'd have the kind of dramatic subject that Alice Cooper might use, but then look at kind of an interior monologue, the way Randy Newman might do it. And so I thought, 'Let's see if we can get inside this guy's head'. So we're not going to talk about the violence or anything like that, but we'll just get inside this guy's kind of muddled-up, slightly twisted thoughts.

A significant part of what makes the song so recognizable is the opening bass line: seven quick evenly-spaced plucks of the A note followed by a quick E and G, then the part immediately repeats. It's simple yet ominous, and the bass is a pounding reminder of the narrator's madness throughout.

In verse one, the speaker admits he 'Can't seem to face up to the facts' and that he can't sleep because his 'bed's on fire'. There are echoes of The Ramones' 'Chain Saw', but this psycho killer is not a cartoon character. Instead, Byrne suggests rather than states his madness, which makes his character seem genuinely menacing, especially after verse two, where he fixates on people who talk too much: 'Say something once/Why say it again?' There's a bit of tongue-in-cheek irony here, of course, coming from a singer-songwriter who's been repeating choruses and verses throughout the album.

The chorus itself is a surprising *mélange*. The singer appears to out himself as a psycho killer in the opening line, then – 'Pourquoi?' – he breaks into French: 'Qu'est-ce que c'est?' We wonder what he means by 'What is this?' Next comes a run of the nonsense syllables we've heard throughout the record, though Byrne has suggested in interviews that there is an allusion to Otis Redding's 'Fa-Fa-Fa-Fa-Fa (Sad Song)'. Then the singer advises someone (Us? His victim? Himself?') to 'Run run run run run run run away'. Not content to make his point once ('Why say it again?'), he repeats the incantation in the second half of the chorus.

In *Remain In Love*, Frantz claims that the song was written in his painting studio at RISD with Weymouth. While the exact line attributions may be hazy, all agree that Weymouth wrote the French bridge lines. On *Fresh Air*, Byrne said he envisioned that the psycho killer 'would imagine himself as very erudite and sophisticated, and so he would sometimes speak in French. So I went to Tina, who had grown up some of the time in Brittany – and her mother is French – and I said, 'Oh, can you help me? We want him to say something pretty grand here, but say it in French as if he's going to tell us what kind of ambitions and how he sees himself'. Roughly translated, the lines are: 'What I did that night/What she said that night/Realizing my hope/I launch towards glory'. Then, in English, the singer throws down the gauntlet, possibly just before his next kill: 'I hate people when they're not polite'.

The chorus repeats and then the song ends with the music mirroring the speaker's madness – the guitars jittering and not quite making sense anymore. Clearly, something unpleasant is happening in those final moments before the song ends on a held chord with a hint of feedback.

'**Pulled Up**' (Byrne)

Talking Heads: 77 could have easily ended with the nightmarish intensity of 'Psycho Killer', the group closing with its signature song. But this remarkable album has one more trick up its sleeve. Throughout, the ebullience of the music has often been at war with the dour complexity of the lyrics, and 'Pulled Up' is one final statement of just how well that formula works. As musically exuberant as any song on the record, the track enters with a crash of cymbals and hurdles forward on bass, drums and Byrne's 'Oh oh oh's. But of course, Talking Heads lyrics are never simple, and as the singer beckons 'Mommy, Daddy, come and look at me now', we wonder how old – mentally at least – this person is, and is he really 'A big man in a great big town', or is that belief purely imaginary? Soon, we learn that the reason he feels he's doing so well despite having 'slipped' and been 'down in the dumps' is because someone has pulled him up, up, up. But who is doing the pulling? His parents? A lover? A friend? An alternate personality? For a while, it doesn't matter. Byrne's manic energy is so contagious it can't be contained by mere words but explodes into 'Na na na's and 'Aye ya ya's. Then, just when it seems the song has said all it's going to say, there comes a verse that practically screams that all, in fact, is *not* right:

I cast a shadow on the living room wall
Dark and savage with a profile so sharp
Keep that wonderful food on the table
There's really no hurry
I'll eat in a while

It's now clear that for all his love of syllabic gibberish, Byrne, in his own odd way, is already a lyricist as original as any of the greats that have preceded him in rock and roll: Bob Dylan, Joni Mitchell, Lennon & McCartney, Lou Reed.

After the final minute of music, the 'pulling up' and incoherent screaming finally end. Most first-time listeners (back in 1977, I was one of them) flipped the record back over and lowered the stylus to the vinyl, eager to figure out what the hell had just happened and to hear it all again.

More Songs About Buildings And Food (1978)

Personnel:
David Byrne: lead vocals, guitars, synthesized percussion
Chris Frantz: drums, percussion
Jerry Harrison: piano, organ, synthesizer, guitar, backing vocals
Tina Weymouth: bass
Brian Eno: synthesizer, piano, guitar, percussion, backing vocals
Tina and the Typing Pool (Tina Weymouth and women working at Compass
Point Studios): backing vocals on 'The Good Thing'
Producers: Brian Eno, Talking Heads
Recorded: March-April 1978
Studio: Compass Point, Nassau
Release date: 14 July 1978
Running time: 41:32
Label: Sire
Album charts: US: 29, UK: 21
Singles charts: 'Take Me To The River', US: 26

The songs on Talking Heads' second album are basically those that didn't make
it to the first album. It would be wrong to call them B-sides or outtakes, for
these numbers had long been part of the band's live set. Frantz wrote in
Remain In Love: 'The songs we were about to record had all been written long
before, mostly before Jerry joined the band. We had been performing them live
on tour. Our playing was very tight and well-rehearsed', as well it might have
been since they 'had played most of these songs hundreds of times'.

Given that these were songs that hadn't made the cut for *Talking Heads: 77*,
the band's sophomore album – like those of so many of their rock 'n' roll
predecessors – could have been a disappointment, a pale imitation of the
first. But Talking Heads never did the same thing twice. Which band member
exactly contacted Brian Eno – whom they had met during their summer 1977
European tour with The Ramones – is a matter of conjecture. But in *How
Music Works*, Byrne gives the whole group credit for inviting Eno into the
fold: 'We liked his music, so we asked ourselves 'Why not have him be our
producer? At least he gets what we're about, and we're already friends'. Byrne
notes that Eno wanted to capture their sound as a live band, so Eno
eliminated many of the physical barriers that studios use to ensure the
separation of instruments: 'Removing some of the sound-absorbent stuff
meant that you could hear the faint sound of guitars in the background of the
drum tracks, and maybe an electric piano might be audible in the background
of the bass track'. But Eno and the band agreed that 'The comfort factor more
than compensated for this technical challenge'.

More Songs About Buildings And Food was the first album ever recorded at
Chris Blackwell's soon-to-be-legendary Island Studios in the Bahamas, so it's
no surprise that the vibe was a good one. In *Remain In Love*, Frantz echoes

Byrne's description of the recording process as going smoothly: 'The mood was very upbeat throughout the sessions. We were all on cloud nine, including Brian, and the energy level was high. We sailed through the recording of the basic tacks in the first ten days. We did multiple takes but usually chose the second or third as the final'. And what exactly was Eno's job as a producer? – a role he held for their next two albums? Ken Emerson describes it succinctly in his *Rolling Stone* review of the album: Eno has 'crammed so much humor and energy into each song. The cerebral, brittle sound of *Talking Heads:* 77 has been fleshed out with supple synthesizer fills, and Chris Frantz's drums and synthesized percussion leap boldly out of the mix. Almost every cut has a percussive gimmick – handclaps, clattering rimshots, a heavily echoed backbeat – that rivets attention, punctuating the melody or hammering home the words'.

One of the less positive results of Eno's production is that – compared to the first album – the vocals are sometimes buried in the mix, making the riffs more memorable than the words. Also, with the notable exception of the final track, 'The Big Country', the lyrics are less complex and less impressive.

Credit for the album title is variously claimed by Weymouth, Frantz and Andy Partridge of XTC, but the general idea that *someone* remarked that these were more songs about buildings and food makes sense, as the tracks are so closely related to their already recorded cousins. And, of course, it's a catchy title because it so obviously thumbs its nose at commercial rock. Who, after all, would want to listen to songs about buildings and food?

Quite a few people, it turned out. The album – released in July 1978 – made the top 30 in the US and the UK, and its surprise hit single 'Take Me To The River' reached number 26 on the *Billboard* Hot 100. Not surprisingly, *Rolling Stone*, *NME*, *Creem* and *The Village Voice* all had good things to say about the record. Even *People* magazine had kind words in their year-end roundup of the best albums of 1978: 'Unlike the rest of the new wave bands, Talking Heads deliver'.

As for the striking cover showing each band member as a composite of separate photos against a red background, Frantz wrote in *Remain In Love*, 'David and Tina took the Polaroid photos that formed the mosaic of the band on the album cover. This was done on the roof of our loft building in Long Island City. Everybody loved the cover, but later, I realized it was heavily influenced by Andrea Kovac's work. We should have given her credit for that'. Kovac was not at all happy about the front cover, though she apparently had no objection to the back cover, which shows Portrait USA.: the first satellite color photo mosaic of the United States from space. It is – as the album's final song proclaims – a 'big country'.

'Thank You For Sending Me An Angel' (Byrne)

The first song chugs into motion on a catchy drum and keyboard riff that hangs on the same chord for 20 seconds before Byrne sings what sounds like words from an old blues single: 'Baby, you can walk/You can talk just like me' and 'You can look/You won't see nothing like me/If you look around the world'. At times, the singing is buried in the mix, which isn't dissimilar to Phil Spector's wall-of-sound technique, where individual instruments are sublimated in service of one grand and wonderful noise.

Nonsense syllables precede a second verse that plays a slight variation on the first, with the singer encouraging his *protégé* ('With a little practice, you can walk, you can talk just like me') and bragging about his own prowess ('But first I'll walk circles 'round you').

Byrne's funky rhythm guitar acts as the solo instrument after verse two, with the final verse serving up yet more variations on walking and talking, circles and going around the world. The repetitive and largely unoriginal lyric is sure to be something of a disappointment to listeners primed on *Talking Heads: 77*. However, it's not the words that strike the listener, but the insistence of the music of this short song, which ends abruptly a little more than two minutes after it began.

'With Our Love' (Byrne)
'With Our Love' begins with the same frenetic energy of the prior track and feels almost like a continuation of it. Short single notes accompany verse one; the music then mellows briefly for the first line of the pre-chorus before the guitars stomp along with Byrne's assertion that the quivering boys from the opening line 'want to forget'.

The chorus toggles back and forth between A and E, and G and E. The music feels as unsettled as the singer sounds – he now has other things to do, though evidently, he's forgotten what they are. Indeed, his memory is so bad that he's forgotten the trouble, which *is* the trouble with his love. At the end of the chorus, the music shifts to something smoother, led by keyboards and bass.

Then the opening riff returns and it's time for part two, with the verses now twice as long. Several ideas familiar from the first album recur: the speaker's mysterious 'friends' (Do they really exist?) and polysyllabic abstractions: in this case, 'education' and 'sophistication'. The rest of the song follows the pattern of part one, with the singer sounding increasingly desperate and off-balance until he ends on an almost Elvis-like 'lu-uh-uh-uh-uve'.

One of Eno's key additions to the album was to treat or alter the sounds of the instruments. Here and elsewhere, Frantz sounds like he could be playing an electric kit and Weymouth's bass resounds with a smooth, almost synthesized flair.

'The Good Thing' (Byrne)
In a 2023 interview with NPR's Steve Inskeep, Byrne discussed the signs that suggested to him he was on the autism spectrum: 'Maybe being slightly socially uncomfortable, or not picking up on the signs when you're engaging

Talking Heads ... *On Track*

with people. Being very able to focus on something, whether it's something you're writing or whatever, and just being very intently focused on that. So there's an upside to it sometimes'. That intense focus, coupled with a lack of ability to register social cues, is evident in most of Byrne's early writing and performing, and it's certainly unmistakable on this album. It manifests in 'The Good Thing' in lines like 'In my mind the weather never changes' (lack of social awareness) and 'A straight line exists between me and the good thing' (intense focus.) The 'straight line' may also refer to the lines in flow charts. Byrne says in *The Band And Their Music* that he 'had been reading a lot of books about systems theory and management theory ... and how the creative process can be broken down into almost a computer flow chart ... It's a philosophy that tends to be very mechanistic, and I found that fascinating for a while'.

It sounds like rather dour subject matter, but the song opens with what you could almost call a *happy* solo guitar figure, accompanied by drums and bass. The sonic landscape of the first verse is cleaner, closer to *Talking Heads: 77*. But the chorus changes all that. Suddenly, a group of singers accompany Byrne for the first time on a Talking Heads album. The credit goes to Tina and the Typing Pool: Tina Weymouth and the female office staff at Island Studios. In *Remain In Love*, Frantz wrote, 'The idea was that they would somehow sound like Chinese youth in the days of Chairman Mao, and, amazingly, they did!' That's a fairly loose description, but with Harrison's electric piano playing, the chorus does sound very different from the verse.

After the second chorus, the song shifts into funk mode, with Byrne claiming, 'I have adopted this and made it my own/Cut back the weakness/ Reinforce what is strong'. The lyric feels genuinely affirmative, even if he is referencing the language of systems management. When he asks us to watch him work, the bass is there to assist as he dives deeper and deeper into 'Work, work/Oh, work!'

'Warning Sign' (Byrne, Frantz)
The bass-forward sound at the end of 'The Good Thing' continues in 'Warning Sign'. However, if the singer had apparently achieved some hard-fought stability in the former song, here he comes across as demented, an amped-up version of his 'Psycho Killer' character.

Byrne doesn't start singing until more than a minute in. First, a catchy bass riff is accompanied by the 'synthesized percussion' effects on Frantz's drums. Guitars and synthesizer then accompany the riff. When the vocal begins, things get weird immediately. While Byrne hears the warning sign, he pays it no mind. Similarly, the voice he hears is 'Saying something, and it's not very nice'. The conversation that unfolds seems to take place partly between the narrator and another of his personas and partly with a woman who may or may not be unconscious or dead: 'Your glassy eyes and your open mouth'. In addition to the voices troubling him, the singer is obsessed with his own hair:

28

'Look at my hair, I like the design/It's the truth, it's the truth'. And then later, 'Hear my voice, move my hair/I move it around a lot/But I don't care what I remember'.

This is one of the earliest Byrne/Frantz collaborations, written in 1973 when they performed as The Artistics, so it makes sense that the speaker's strangeness would be over the top. In a video of 'Warning Sign' played by the pre-Harrison Talking Heads at CBGB, Byrne just looks nervous, not dangerous at all. But Eno's big, professional production, which includes a voice periodically demanding 'What is it?' ('Qu'est-ce que c'est?' we recall the psycho killer asking) gives the track a schizophrenic menace.

'The Girls Want To Be With The Girls' (Byrne)

Many of Byrne's early lyrics about romance feel juvenile, and this song brings that dynamic to the forefront. Weymouth seems to confirm Byrne's naivete in *The Band And Their Music*: 'I couldn't believe it when I saw it: the words were all verbatim out of a conversation David and I had. He was learning that girls are just like boys – sometimes it's reassuring for girls to be with other girls in each other's company. It's not because they're sitting in the corner laughing at the boys'.

The track starts with a two-chord riff over a 4/4 rhythm. A simple bass line and Harrison's twinkling piano give the verse a feeling of innocence, as the singer lets us know that girls 'Just want to do what's in their hearts'. The lyric in the answering verse is actually 'And the boys say 'What do you mean?' but the line is easily misheard as 'And the boys just want to be mean', a sentiment that's surely buried not too deeply in the lyric. In any event, the singer sums up his philosophy succinctly in the line, 'Well, there's just no love when there's boys and girls'. It's a depressing, simplistic view of the relationship between men and women. Granted, Byrne clearly sees the girls as superior to the boys. 'Girls want things that make common sense/The best for all concerned'. Moreover, 'Girls are getting into abstract analysis/Would like to make that intuitive leap'. Meanwhile, the dimwitted boys keep asking, 'What do you mean?' It's always hard to tell with Byrne, but Weymouth's observation notwithstanding, there does seem to be at least a modicum of tongue-in-cheek humor beneath Byrne's highly-pitched, deadpan delivery.

The rat-tat-tat rhythm guitar, combined with the soaring keyboards, make for a fun piece of music, but, as ever, Byrne's lyrics complicate the good times.

'Found A Job' (Byrne)

Side one concludes with 'Found A Job', which begins almost immediately after the previous track. A new listener without recourse to a track list might initially think this is a continuation of 'The Girls Want to Be with the Girls'. However, that impression is soon dispelled despite the continuing energetic rhythm guitars, adamant bass line and sure-handed drumming. We're thrown headfirst into a narrative about Bob and Judy – two people who fight over what's on television and otherwise waste their precious time until they take the singer's advice to make up 'their own shows which might be better than TV'. (In *The Band And Their Music*, Byrne said, 'I wrote that song when I went to visit my parents, and some of the lines are taken from an argument I had there'.)

After the two initial verses, the chorus arrives: 'Judy's in the bedroom, inventing situations', while 'Bob is on the street today, scouting up locations'. Apparently, in the span of a few seconds, the warring couple has made the transition to becoming television stars. Soon, we learn that 'Their show gets real high ratings/They think they have a hit/There might even be a spin-off/But they're not sure 'bout that'. The bottom line is – as the singer assures us towards the end – 'If your work isn't what you love/Then something isn't right'.

Writing in *Hyperallergic*, Lucas Fagen noted that the 'thumpy bass, percussive rhythm guitar, and exuberant chord progression would sound like funk if the guitars weren't so harsh, so cutting, so mechanical'. But of course, that's the *point* of a Talking Heads song – to take old materials and make them new, even if it means breaking some things along the way.

'Artists Only' (Byrne, Zieve)

In their next two albums – *Fear Of Music* and *Remain In Light* – Talking Heads focused more on making music as a band rather than simply fleshing out Byrne's odd and inventive lyric fantasies. 'Artists Only' suggests what the ensemble as a group of *musicians* might become.

The brief lyric consists of three verses, each consisting of variations on a single statement. 1: 'I'm painting, I'm painting again'; 2: 'Pretty soon now, I will be bitter'; 3: 'I don't have to prove that I am creative!' The voice sounds like that of a flailing, egomaniacal art student: a character the Rhode Island School of Design alums would be very familiar with. In fact, in *The Band And Their Music*, Byrne states that the lyric was 'someone else's words that were written for a song, sort of a found thing'. The words are courtesy of Wayne Zieve, who is also credited with coming up with the group's name. Byrne continues: 'I thought it would be interesting to construct a song with long instrumental passages and quickly get the words over with'. Indeed, in between the lyric screeds, a lovely, intriguing guitar-keyboard counterpoint plays over a no-nonsense bass and drum part before all four instruments combine. There's a distorted guitar solo after verse one; after verse two, the opening figure returns and is extended into more distorted guitar, followed by organ. The outro is the intro played at an increasingly slower tempo.

Journalist Mikal Gilmore opined that the song was 'as visceral a display as is called for in rock and roll. Byrne and Harrison interweave peppered and eruptive bursts of melody that skitter madly across Chris and Tina's immutable, mesmerizing rhythm lines. But in spite of Jerry and David's disclaimers, I feel very much that it has a foot in art: sinewy, rumbling, kinetic art'.

'I'm Not In Love' (Byrne)

In *Once In A Lifetime*, Ian Gittins says of the persona conjured up by Talking Heads' singer: 'Wired and independent, perennially checking his back, Byrne always seems like someone pathologically unwilling or unable to subjugate his ego in an equal relationship with a partner'. While this is certainly true of 'I'm Not in Love' and most of Byrne's oeuvre, music rather than lyrics are at the forefront in this song.

The track begins with a catchy guitar/keyboard riff played twice before Frantz machine-guns in and the drums become a huge driving presence until two lines in. When the music pauses, Byrne sings a line so low you can barely hear it: 'We are two strangers we might never have met'. The music starts and hangs on a chord as Byrne sings over the semi-silence, and the music and lyrics toggle back and forth to the end of the chorus. ('Do people really fall in love?') The process repeats, and after the second chorus, Byrne's manic rhythm guitar leads to one last verse with a chorus variation ('I believe that we don't need love').

Then, with a minute and 45 seconds left, 'I'm Not In Love' becomes the sort of dance-friendly workout jam that came to characterize so much later Talking Heads music. The bass grows more dominant as the guitar licks come in time with Frantz's driving rhythms. This is now a *band* grooving, not three backing players accompanying a singer.

'Stay Hungry' (Byrne, Frantz)

Another extremely short break between tracks makes 'Stay Hungry' feel like the third song in a musical trilogy. A frenetic guitar introduction and a two-line opening verse give way to a mellow passage that serves as a kind of chorus. The lyric consists of phrases sung three times over the course of eight lines: 'Stay hungry, stay hungry, stay hungry', 'Move a muscle, move a muscle, move a muscle', etc. In *This Must Be The Place*, David Bowman says the words 'came from a muscle magazine Chris saw on a newsstand'. The lyric is akin to sound poetry, where meaning is subservient to the pure pleasure of phonetics.

When the chorus ends, the funk begins. The band stays with a single E-minor chord for 45 seconds, with the only variation being the pace of Byrne's strumming and the three-and-four-note bass line. Finally, Harrison enters with a mysteriously soothing synthesizer part, and Byrne sings about the return of the rhythm as the song fades out.

'Take Me To The River' (Green, Hodges)

This track's opening is so familiar to most listeners of popular music that it's hard to convey just how strange and fresh it sounded on car radios back in 1978. If you had heard of Talking Heads at all, it was probably because of 'Psycho Killer': a persona that Byrne did a remarkable job of inhabiting. But 'Take Me To The River' was different: still weird, but almost bluesy for a New Wave band. When the bass entered ten seconds in, you were hooked.

In *Remain In Light*, Frantz says the band had been playing the song faster, but that Eno suggested they play it as slow as they could, and the result was this sinuous, some even say *sexy* version. Harrison's organ playing is a highlight throughout, playing the hook and teasing and challenging Byrne's strong vocal.

Al Green's original version, augmented by strings and horns, was faster than this version, and his famously soulful voice was clearly superior to Byrne's, though both are tenors. The elliptical storyline (the singer seems to have had a sexual breakthrough with his 'sweet sixteen', but his lover is now treating him 'so bad') is in keeping with Byrne's own lyrics about dysfunctional love.

Despite undoubtedly being a signature song, in a 2020 *Songfacts* interview, Frantz explained why this was the band's first and only cover song: 'David got mad – this is so David Byrne. He got mad that the hit was not one of his songs … When that happened, it meant we could get a lot of gigs that we couldn't have gotten as an unknown band, and everything started to move a lot faster for us. But David resented that it wasn't one of his songs that was the hit. So he said, 'I'm not doing any more cover songs'.'

'The Big Country' (Byrne)

As was the case with *Talking Heads: 77*, *More Songs About Buildings And Food* could have easily ended with the single, but the fact that neither album took the easy route paid off again. The second album's closing track, 'The Big Country', offered Byrne's strongest lyric and most convincing vocal performance to that point.

The song takes its time getting started, with a languid slide guitar played over the classic country-and-western chords C/D/F/G. In his contribution to the 33 1/3 series, *Fear Of Music* author Jonathan Lethem reckoned that 'The slide guitar can be taken two ways – a satirical gesture, furthering the song's atmosphere of scorn by framing a sound that's emblematically *corny*, or a preemptive musical apology for the slight'. That scorn becomes readily apparent as soon as Byrne begins singing, when we realize 'the big country' isn't some hoedown at the Grand Ol' Opry, but rather a description of the United States: 'I see the shapes I remember from maps'. Perhaps because he's singing in a slightly lower register, as Byrne deconstructs the countryside he sees from his airplane window, he sounds less frantic, less crazy than in other songs. Despite his evident disdain for 'baseball diamonds' and 'places to park by the factories and buildings', he acknowledges that 'The air is clean' and 'Those people have fun with their neighbors and friends'. (And 'friends', as we know, mean a lot to Byrne.)

Still, this is a far cry from the willful naivete of 'Don't Worry About The Government'. What makes the 'The Big Country' so different, not only from the album's other tracks and, indeed, from most of the band's overall oeuvre, is the glimmer of an actual human being that Byrne allows to peek through in the chorus. He tells us, 'I wouldn't live there if you paid me', and you can hear the bitter certainty of that statement in the voice of the boy who fled suburban Maryland for New York City.

Unfortunately, towards the end, Byrne transitions into baby talk. Perhaps the point was to emphasize the infantilism of the people he's been describing – after all, he claims it's 'those people down there' who are making the puerile noises – but the effect is to undercut the seriousness of the critique he's just made of consumerism and middle-class life. In a 2023 interview with Este Haim, Weymouth lamented the song's conclusion: 'It starts off very melodic, but then the chorus just totally takes the piss out because it's just like 'Goo-goo, ga-ga-ga'. It's just horrible. That was the point of it, I suppose. That was a jerk point of view, but it's super limited and narrow'. And yet, even if the baby talk passage is a mistake, the outro is wordless and guitar-driven, concluding with a rather traditional solo. When the song is over, we tend to recall not so much the 'horrible' part that bothers Weymouth but the breadth of vision in the lyric and the genuine sincerity of a man who 'is tired of traveling' and wants 'to be somewhere'.

Talking Heads ... *On Track*

Fear Of Music (1979)

Personnel:
David Byrne: lead vocals, guitar; backing vocals ('I Zimbra')
Jerry Harrison: guitar, backing vocals, keyboards
Tina Weymouth: bass, backing vocals
Chris Frantz: drums
Brian Eno: treatments; backing vocals ('I Zimbra'); additional vocals
Gene Wilder: congas ('I Zimbra', 'Life During Wartime')
Ari: congas ('I Zimbra', 'Life During Wartime')
Robert Fripp: guitar ('I Zimbra')
The Sweetbreathes (Lani Weymouth, Laura Weymouth, Tina Weymouth): backing vocals ('Air')
Julie Last: backing vocals ('I Zimbra')
Hassam Ramzy: surdo ('I Zimbra')
Abdou M'Boup: djembe, talking drum ('I Zimbra')
Assane Thiam: percussion ('I Zimbra')
Producers: Brian Eno, Talking Heads
Release date: 3 August 1979
Recorded: April 22 and May 6, 1979
Studios: Chris and Tina's loft, Long Island City; Hit Factory, Atlantic, R.P.M., and Record Plant, New York City
Running time: 40:40
Label: Sire
Album charts: US: 21, UK: 33
Singles charts: 'Life During Wartime', US: 80

Like The Beatles, Talking Heads retained a recognizable sound while growing with each album. Granted, tension was already emerging between Byrne and Weymouth, who felt the frontman was getting all the credit while the band that made him sound so good was often ignored. But there was no serious talk of breaking up at this point, despite occasional rumors that Byrne was leaving Talking Heads. In a 2022 interview, Harrison told *Glide* magazine's Leslie Michele Derrough, '*Fear Of Music*, I always thought, was the culmination of us as a four-piece because we had become better and better players from touring. I don't know, there's something just extremely special about that'.

An episode of the English TV show *South Bank* (available on YouTube) spends time with Talking Heads in Frantz and Weymouth's loft in Long Island City, Queens, after the completion of *Fear Of Music*. It's hard to imagine the place as the recording location of what many rock critics call one of the best albums of the decade. The loft is bare and kind of messy – about what you'd expect of the living space of a childless, arty couple in their late 20s. Nevertheless, this is where it happened (Eno's extensive post-production work notwithstanding). On 22 April and 6 May 1979, the mobile engineering

34

crew of the Record Plant parked their truck downstairs and ran cables up to the third-floor loft. Frantz described the process in *Remain In Love*: 'After we got a good sound on all the instruments, we played each song as if we were playing a live show. Brian sat in the mini control room in the truck with engineer Rod O'Brian, who recorded everything. We had been working on these songs for weeks, and our playing was really energetic and tight'.

But before the songs could be completed, they needed lyrics and vocals, which was an issue for Byrne. The first two albums had exhausted him of original songs, and unlike Bob Dylan or Bruce Springsteen, Byrne wasn't someone to sit down and pound out lyrics. In fact, his true lyrical element wasn't so much the song or even the verse or chorus but the *line*. In *How Music Works*, he acknowledged that 'Recording songs that were incomplete was risky for me. I wondered could I really create a song by singing over prerecorded riffs and chord changes?' This process of music first and lyrics later proved to be a game-changer for Byrne's future composition strategies. He learned he was 'able to write words that responded to and were guided by prerecorded music, instead of getting all bent out of shape trying to get the music to fit – not just melodically, but sonically and texturally – pre-written lyrics'.

In *The Band And Their Music*, Harrison says that the idea for the album title *Fear Of Music* emerged during the recording of the previous album: 'David was talking about a book he had been reading called *Music And The Brain*. There is a particular type of epilepsy that is set off by music ... I said, 'Boy, that would be a great name for an album'. We all laughed and said it would be great, and it just sort of stuck'.

Harrison was also instrumental in the cover design, although, in *The Band And Their Music,* Byrne doesn't hesitate to take some of the credit: 'The cover was mainly Jerry's idea. He originally wanted to use a different material – some sort of plastic – but that was too expensive. I designed the typeface, where it should go, how big it should be and the layout. It was rubber flooring, but it's the same pattern used on metal'. In fact, the cover was, of course, made of cardboard, but it was an arresting and tactile design, so much so that the back cover simply consisted of the black tread with 'Produced by Brian Eno and Talking Heads' in tiny green letters at the bottom.

Released in August 1979, the new Talking Heads album – like those before it – became a critical darling. Jon Parles wrote in his *Rolling Stone* review: 'Whereas *More Songs About Buildings And Food* was crisp and outgoing, *Fear Of Music* is often deliberately, brilliantly disorienting. Like its black, corrugated packaging (which resembles a manhole cover), the album is foreboding, inescapably urban and obsessed with texture'.

In his book on *Fear Of Music* in Bloomsbury's 33 1/3 series, Jonathan Lethem intersperses his discussion of individual tracks with questions about the nature of the album overall. 'Is it a Talking Heads Record?' he asks. His answer: 'In some ways, it may be the last Talking Heads record'. Is it 'a David

Byrne album?' Responding to himself, he says: 'No matter your investment in the premise of a collective entity known as Talking Heads, we're forced here to pause and admit that this band has a clear leader'.

In fact, the answer to the questions Lethem asks about the album is always a qualified 'Yes', so let us list those questions here: 'Is *Fear Of Music* a text?' 'Is *Fear Of Music* a New York album?' 'Is *Fear Of Music* a science fiction record?' 'Is *Fear Of Music* a paranoid record?' Perhaps most intriguingly, Lethem asks, 'Is *Fear Of Music* an Asperger's record?' His reply is the kind of generous response that Byrne and others who have been classified with the syndrome deserve. Lethem writes:

It might be worth keeping in mind … that Asperger's and the whole autism *spectrum* is only a local prevailing condition in the history of human self-understanding … We locate so much Asperger's Syndrome right now everywhere, in ourselves and children and our art, at least partly because it gives the relief of a name to one of the unnameable zones in the contemporary relation of our curious, helpless minds, to the stuff outside of our minds, to the problem of buildings and food, and of people.

One other question Lethem could have asked: 'Is *Fear Of Music* a comedy album?' Writing in *The Village Voice*, Lester Bangs seemed to think so. After noting how Byrne 'seems to be a kind of dowser's wand to neuroses and trauma', Bangs calls *Fear Of Music* 'one of the best comedy albums I've heard'. Reviewing the album in *Pitchfork* decades later, Jayson Greene agreed: 'The album plays like a series of mini standup routines about the absurdity or the pointlessness of human observation'.

At one point in the 1979 *South Bank* TV show episode, while rehearsing for a gig, Harrison forgets a guitar line, and Frantz puts a copy of the album on the record player. As he lowers the stylus and the distinctive gold and blue Sire logo begins spinning around, one can't help but think how low-tech Talking Heads' resources seem now and how amazing it was that the band, with Eno's considerable assistance, was able to produce a sonic masterpiece.

'I Zimbra' (Byrne, Eno, Ball)

The album's first track was actually the last completed. With its conga-heavy African rhythms (thanks to two street musicians Byrne drafted from Washington Square Park), the song begins with dueling, funky rhythm guitars punctuated by emphatic bass notes.

But what in the world is Byrne singing? Many Anglophone listeners assumed the song was a translation from a language like Swahili or Hausa, and, rhythmically speaking, they would have been in the ballpark. In *The Band And Their Music*, Byrne says the song 'was inspired by an African record called 'Seventeen Mabone' by the Makgona Tsohle Band.

While Talking Heads and their producer all loved the track's music, Byrne couldn't come up with a satisfactory lyric. Finally, Eno suggested that Byrne sing 'Gadji beri bimb': a Dada poem written by Hugo Ball in 1916. Byrne, of course, had already made extensive use of 'non-lexical vocables': the 'na na na's and other invented phrases on the first two albums. Moreover, combining random words and phrases was hardly new (think of The Beatles' 'I Am The Walrus', or Elton John's 'Solar Prestige A Gammon'). Yet, Talking Heads infused an incredible urgency into these absurdist lines, which made them feel as much like a political statement as Dylan's 'Blowin' In The Wind'. It is appropriate that Hugo Ball got a writing credit, but Eno's mere suggestion of a poem might leave some questioning Eno's writing credit.

In addition to the congas and Frantz's usual stellar drumming, the percussion is driven by world musicians Hassam Ramzy on surdo (a bass drum), Adbou M'Boup on djembe (a rope-tuned goblet drum) and Assane Thiam on a variety of instruments. Robert Fripp's slippery guitar line weaves through the song, adding an air of mystery. The vocal ensemble accompanying Byrne gives the number an uplifting tribal feel. The singers consisted of Weymouth, her sisters Lani and Laura (billed as The Sweetbreathes), Harrison, Eno and assistant engineer Julie Last. It's a group effort, to be sure.

On *Remain In Light*, songwriting credits were to become a major issue, with Weymouth, Frantz and Harrison insisting on being acknowledged, and much of that conflict had to do with the successful creation of 'I Zimbra', where Byrne only credited Eno and Ball as co-authors. The song began as a band jam, a process that the band found particularly compelling. In a 1997 interview with *Liquid Audio*, Harrison remarked that they 'knew that our next album would be a further exploration of what we had begun with 'I Zimbra'.'

'Mind' (Byrne)

'Mind' changes the vibe into something considerably more mellow. Despite the busy guitar part, unexpectedly-placed bass notes and off-the-wall synthesizer sound effects, Frantz's steady drumming holds everything together. In *Remain In Love*, he proudly notes that The Clash's Joe Strummer once called him 'a proper drummer'. And Jon Parles pointed out in his *Rolling Stone* review that 'Frantz will sometimes hold one lick for an entire cut. For example, the steady hi-hat 8th notes he plays throughout 'Mind'. It's deliberately mechanical, but because the riffs are complexly intertwined and there's a solid backbeat, the repetition doesn't inspire Kraftwerk-style boredom or disco claustrophobia. Instead, there's a sense of time being held at bay'.

The verse lyrics list the number of things that are *not* going to change the mind of the person being addressed: time, money, drugs, religion and science. It sounds like a hopeless case, and the singer admits he hasn't 'got the faintest idea' about things, and anyway, his beloved is 'not even listening' to him.

Meanwhile, the chorus consists of a single repeated line: 'I need something to change your mind'. In the second and third choruses, 'mind' is repeated at the end in a slightly different voice, as though the singer is talking to himself or someone is talking to him.

A growling, if simple guitar solo with actual distortion takes out the final 55 seconds in a slow fade-out that seems to echo the singer's unwillingness to realize he's never going to change the mind of the person in the song.

'Paper' (Byrne)

Over three albums, David Byrne had written some of the strangest love songs in popular music, and 'Paper' certainly falls into that category. The song's high-energy funk riff, one of the catchiest on the album, is in keeping with 'I Zimbra', but initially, it's difficult to get a handle on the subject matter. 'Hold the paper up to the light/Some rays pass right through', Byrne sings. And the next two first-verse lines hardly clarify matters: 'Expose yourself out there for a minute/Some rays pass right through'.

In his book on *Fear Of Music*, Jonathan Lethem makes a case for the song as enacting 'an artistic crisis, possibly even disclosing a blatantly embarrassing case of writer's block. The harder you try to parse the lyrics, the more they resemble a vortex of notes – pages flying off a calendar'.

Granted, the lyrics are rife with Byrnian ambiguity, but halfway through, as the music begins to repeat the patterns of the first half, we learn that the piece of paper is actually an implied metaphor for a romance that went south: 'Had a love affair, but it was only paper'. It's hardly a Shakespearian metaphor, but suddenly those rays passing 'right through' gain some symbolic heft, and when in the final verse the singer decides to 'Rip up, rip up the paper', we realize that he's more than just a disgruntled office worker removing a sheet of paper from the copy machine.

'Cities' (Byrne)

'Cities' fades in with what could be a siren and the increasingly loud sound of military drumming. Then, over an upbeat barrage of rhythm guitars and a four-note bass figure, Byrne begins singing: 'Think of London, small city/It's dark, dark in the daytime'. Whatever London was at the end of the 1970s, it wasn't small, but the fact that the singer claims it's dark in the daytime takes us back centuries to when the city wasn't actually that large, and fog and smoke could make sunshine feel like a rarity. Indeed, this song's location in the historical timeline is deliberately ambiguous.

Byrne's singing throughout feels desperate. He croaks and squawks some lines as though in dire need of 'a city to live in'. He acknowledges that the process of searching for a home is leaving him 'a little freaked out'. The music lopes along, too frantic to be fun, too bouncy to be dour. The bass drives the narrative forward. But as the song fades into an extended outro, Byrne's singing becomes more aggressive, more disjointed. Our faith in his ability to find a city to live in diminishes with each repeated assertion that he will do so.

However, it's the imagery and wordplay that make the song what it is. Who else but Byrne would claim there are a 'lot of rich people in Birmingham' (well, no, not really), then point out a 'dry ice factory' and note that it's a 'good place to get some thinking done'. Later when he mentions Memphis, we find he's referencing not only the 'home of Elvis', but 'the ancient Greeks'. And when he thinks he smells home cooking, it may be 'only the river'. But *which* river exactly? The Mississippi or the Nile? Or both?

One thing is certain: the singer most definitely does *not* have it 'figured out'. He's searching but confused, doing his best to put up a confident front but clearly failing to convince himself that everything is all right. As Jon Parles wrote in *Rolling Stone*: 'David Byrne's private, paranoid universe is dangerously close to yours and mine'.

'Life During Wartime' (Byrne, Frantz, Harrison, Weymouth)
At least on the CD release (Byrne originally took credit for all songs except 'I Zimbra'), the band finally got co-writing credit for music written during the loft's jam sessions. But while 'Life During Wartime' rests on a punchy, synth-driven riff, what one ultimately remembers most about the song is its narrative. If 'The Big Country' proved that Byrne could handle serious topics in a semi-serious fashion, 'Life During Wartime' showed just how much he'd grown as a lyricist.

After several repetitions of the riff that continues for most of the song, the story begins *in medias res*: 'Heard of a van that is loaded with weapons/ Packed up and ready to go'. From then on, it's one concrete example after another, bringing to life a civilization on the verge of collapse. In previous songs, Byrne might have reverted to comedy to undercut his gravity ('Goo goo, ga ga ga', say), but the closest thing to flippancy comes in the chorus (signaled by a key change from A minor to E major) when he uses terms like 'dancing' and 'lovey-dovey', and later the Mudd Club and CBGB, before declaring 'I ain't got time for that now'.

The song is rife with memorable lines, like 'This ain't no party/This ain't no disco/This ain't no fooling around'. (Byrne recounted in a radio interview that a club owner once strung a big sign across the stage that said 'This Ain't No Disco'. The irony is that 'we liked a lot of disco music, and, in fact, a lot of disco music inspired us'.) Other great lines include 'Lived in a brownstone/ Lived in the ghetto/I've lived all over this town' and 'I've changed my hairstyle so many times now/I don't know what I look like'.

The track has a long fade-out, with Byrne continuing to sing new lyrics into the silence – 'My chest is aching/Burns like a furnace/The burning keeps me alive' – suggesting that his many gambits necessary to survive are not likely to end anytime soon. Explaining why the lyric printed on the sleeve continued past the actual singing, Byrne said in *The Band And Their Music*, 'I wanted to give the impression that it could just go on and on with an endless description of that scene ... It was to give the idea that the song wasn't a story with a beginning and an end, just a description'. (One recalls Elizabeth Bishop's famous dictum: 'Poetry is mostly description'.)

Byrne claimed that the images in 'Life During Wartime' were inspired by living in his apartment on the edge of Tompkins Square Park. But even during the 1970s, Alphabet City was never quite the apocalyptic spectacle the lyrics depict. And there were plenty of real-world instances of desperate people doing desperate things to stay alive: in Cambodia and Zaire, Afghanistan and Angola. However, the song's true inspiration was end-of-the-world novels like George Rippey Stewart's *Earth Abides* (1949) and Stephen King's *The Stand* (1978), as well as movies like *The Omega Man* (1971) and *The Crazies* (1973.) Whether or not Byrne saw the original *Mad Max* movie, it's not surprising that it was released just a few weeks before the album was recorded. Something ominous was in the air.

'Memories Can't Wait' (Byrne, Harrison)

In *Remain In Love*, you can hear Weymouth and Frantz's building resentment against Byrne, as the drummer writes of 'Memories Can't Wait': 'The song began as a jam between Tina and me. The entire song, including the vocal melody, is based on Tina's part ... Though he came up with fantastic lyrics, David later credited himself as the sole writer of the song. This happened all the time with David. He couldn't acknowledge where he stopped and other people began'.

'Memories Can't Wait' begins with a driving guitar riff, and though the chords change during the song, the overall impression is of one single, incessant *pulse*.

The music and lyric are perfectly matched, and what a lyric it is. If Byrne's oeuvre up to this point had been marked by frantic solipsism, in 'Memories Can't Wait', the man who is perpetually living in his own head comes across as both pitiable and poignant. The pre-chorus, with its wry observation that 'There's a party in my mind/And the party never stops', sounds like it will fall in line with the creepy-comic feel of so many prior Talking Heads songs, but – in popular music, at least – there's rarely been a more precise and moving description of what it feels like to be alone with one's thoughts:

Other people can go home
Everybody else will split
I'll be here all the time
I can never quit

The first three parts (it seems just barely permissible to call them verse/pre-chorus/chorus, especially when we know how those terms will be deconstructed in the next album, *Remain In Light*) are repeated with slight variations, and then a coda emerges: 'Everything is very quiet/Everyone has gone to sleep'. But the singer can't go to sleep, he's 'wide awake on memories', and then the title finally appears and is sung five (and a half) times to drive home the intensity of his self-absorbed situation.

In the liner notes for *The Best Of Talking Heads*, Moby wrote:

> Whenever I walk around Chinatown, I think of Talking Heads recording *Fear Of Music* in a hot, sweaty loft next to a sweatshop, and I think of this amazing song. 'Memories Can't Wait' is certainly up there with 'Heroin' by the Velvet Underground and 'The Jean Genie' by David Bowie as great New York drug songs.

In *Once In A Lifetime*, Ian Gittins dismisses the song's 'B-movie melodrama accentuated by reverb-heavy Eno production that makes Byrne's quavering voice resonate as though from some deep, unfathomable abyss', which leads Gittins to conclude that 'Memories Can't Wait' 'now appears a quaint, dated oddity'. I couldn't disagree more. What I hear on this final song of side one is a lament for everything that's come before – on the previous five tracks, yes, but also in the first 27 years of Byrne's complicated and eventful life.

'Air' (Byrne)

Byrne has claimed on a number of occasions that the lyric of 'Air' is not meant to be ironic, yet it is initially hard to take at face value a line like 'Some people never had experience with air'. Yet, on reflection, the line can feel true in a skewed way – surely some people never think about the air they breathe, so they don't *experience* it like the singer. Moreover, the air pollution of the late 1970s was hardly a joke: in many ways, human skin did need protection. Still, the secret sauce in almost any of Byrne's most memorable lyrics is exaggeration, and it is most fruitful to hear his hyperbole as part of the song's dark fun. In *Remain In Love*, Frantz recalled Byrne saying that his Scots grandmother once warned him, "Trust no one, Davy. Even your own asshole will let you down'. I think that's what this song is about'.

'Air' begins with a loping bass line and vocals from The Sweetbreathes, adding a bit of mystery to whatever is coming our way. Initially, the syllable they harmonize on sounds like vocalese. However, by the second iteration, we realize they are singing the song's title. The introduction gives way to a quirky synthesizer patch and the arresting opening line, 'Hit me in the face'. But it's not a fist that's punching the singer – it's the air, which he claims 'can hurt you too'.

The half-comical synthesizer returns as Byrne tells us air 'can break your heart', undercutting the warning's supposed seriousness. Nevertheless, when he asks, 'What is happening to my skin?' the music shifts into major chords that seem sweet and sincere. The minute-long outro, which features a guitar solo working with and against the backing vocals, makes the song feel longer

Talking Heads ... *On Track*

than its three and a half minutes, as though we have been asked to join the experience of the singer's endless battle with the air.

'Heaven' (Byrne, Harrison)

The opening chords here suggest we might be in for another country song *à la* 'The Big Country'. Indeed, in *The Band And Their Music*, Byrne says he started 'Heaven' trying to emulate Neil Young, and when Byrne begins singing, he sounds downright mellow, far from the agitated vocals of the first two albums. Harrison's acoustic-piano-playing is melancholy and reassuring.

The music – credited to Byrne and Harrison – is surely one reason for the song's success, but it's the argument of the lyric that is so striking. Essentially, the singer's contention is that the ideal condition for eternity is stasis and repetition: 'It's hard to imagine that nothing at all/Could be so exciting/Could be this much fun'. For someone shy, socially awkward and worn down by the rigors of constant touring and self-promotion, 'A place where nothing ever happens' and 'Everyone leaves at the same time' might indeed seem like Heaven.

But, of course, not everyone found this vision of a perpetually inert Heaven appealing. In *Remain In Love*, the peripatetic Frantz writes, 'The lyrics are pretty cynical, and it's ironic that some people have chosen this as their wedding or funeral song. Can it really be anyone's idea of Heaven that it is a place where nothing ever happens? Weird'.

Nevertheless, 'Heaven' has appealed to a host of other artists, from Eric Burdon to Simply Red to artists singing in German and Swedish. Something about the idea of retreating from novelty and constant action resonates widely. Among the most moving covers of the song are the country-inflected version by K. D. Lang and The National's version on the *Stop Making Sense* tribute album. Perhaps it's an exaggeration to call 'Heaven' a contemporary standard, but it certainly holds up well when performed by a variety of singers, and the original version continues to sound magnificent.

'Animals' (Byrne)

If listeners thought Byrne had a problem with air, they learn in this song that he has an even bigger bugaboo: animals. 'Heaven' shows how far Byrne had come as a serious lyricist, but the gravitational pull of silliness and absurdity was to remain strong for years to come.

The narrator of 'Animals' is a kind of inverse Janina Duszejko, the protagonist of Olga Tokarczuk's *Drive Your Plow Over The Bones Of The Dead*. Tokarczuk's character would do anything to save animals, up to and including murder. But the persona created by Byrne loathes everything about non-human creatures. Part of the gag is Byrne's personification of animals. Not only don't they *help,* but they 'Always let you down, down, down, down'. In addition to never being there when you need them, they offer bad advice and they are always 'laughing at us'. Indeed, the singer gets so worked-up that 'Animals' is one of the rare Byrne compositions that includes a 'vulgar' word: 'Animals think they're pretty smart/Shit on the ground, see in the dark'.

The music is equally off-balance. After a brief introduction, the verse is sung over a chord that switches quickly between major and minor. The effect is to emphasize the weird anger of the shouted lyric. And while there's a brief reprieve in what passes for a chorus, the overall feel is of a song looking for a key to call home.

The final 80 seconds are given to a rant over variations on a single chord, with the singer becoming increasingly agitated as he rails about how 'They think they know what's best/They're making a fool of us'. There is comedy here for sure, but its troubling humor is guaranteed to keep the album from settling into anything resembling a mellow mood.

'Electric Guitar' (Byrne)

'Electric Guitar' continues the return to what might be called the World of Crazy David, where his observations resemble the lines of a surrealist poem. The music is appropriately druggy, with Frantz's drums high in the mix. Speaking to Seattle music magazine *The Rocket* about 'Electric Guitar', Weymouth said 'Eno actually achieved something that I really was pleased with … He put an effect on my bass so that it really sounded like a tuba, and I was real pleased with that'. Indeed, there are faint echoes of the prominent tuba in The Beatles' 'Yellow Submarine', though Byrne's lyric is much stranger than McCartney's.

The singing here is often muddy and hard to decipher, but basically, the song tells the story of an electric guitar that was run over on the highway. Apparently, 'This is a crime against the state' and tuning the electric guitar 'is the meaning of life'. Things get even weirder when the electric guitar is 'brought into a court of law' and a judge and jury sit around listening to records before confirming that this is, in fact, a crime against the state, reaching the verdict 'Never listen to electric guitar'. A five-note run similar to the one heard in 'Animals' accents the accusations against the dastardly electric guitar. Byrne briefly rails against the character assassination of electric guitar, shouting 'No!' before yet another verdict is reached at the end: some unknown personage 'controls electric guitar'.

Finally, with a flourish of drums and a bit of feedback, it's over. As Frantz said of 'Heaven', weird.

'Drugs' (Byrne, Eno)

However, things are about to get even weirder as the closing song – the album's longest – enters with what sounds like birds or crickets. A riff played between bass and guitar, with periodic synthesizer washes, goes on for 90 seconds before there is any singing. Of all the tracks on the album, this one sounds the most like it could be pulled straight from the Eno catalog: perhaps an outtake from *Taking Tiger Mountain (By Strategy)*.

There's an irregular emptiness to the music, which Byrne explained in *How Music Works*: 'We had initially recorded a fairly straightforward backing track that seemed a bit conventional, so we began to mute some of the instruments, sometimes silencing specific notes'. Other unconventional elements of 'Drugs' (originally called 'Electricity') are the grunts and snorts of koalas that Byrne had recorded in Australia, a guitar solo at the end 'made by selecting fragments from a number of improvised solos', and the fact that Byrne 'sang the song after jogging in the studio, because for some reason I wanted to sound out of breath'.

Jon Parles pointed out in his *Rolling Stone* review that the transformation from a song the band had been performing live and calling 'Electricity' to 'Drugs' is a radical one. The earlier version 'was an easygoing, almost country-ish guitar-vamp number. On *Fear Of Music*, Eno and Talking Heads eliminate the vamp, reverse the beat, stick a bell on every downbeat (like Jimmy Cliff's 'Sitting In Limbo'), change some lyrics, rewrite the bridge in a different key, and fill the hole left by the vamp with echoes and strange noises'.

Lyrically, 'Drugs' is a not-too-distant cousin of 'Psycho Killer'. The singer may 'Feel like murder, but that's alright'. He's 'Charged up, it's pretty intense'. The title suggests that drugs are responsible for his behavior (Byrne has said his drug of choice was cocaine), but the sonic landscape makes the singer's disorientation feel brooding, if not downright sinister. What one ultimately remembers is the *mood* of 'Drugs' – it's not a frame of mind most people would want to inhabit for long. 'It could only have been created in a studio', Byrne noted, looking toward his and Eno's collaboration on *My Life In The Bush Of Ghosts* and Talking Heads' fourth album *Remain In Light*. As Eno observed at the time, 'the recording studio was now a compositional tool'.

Talking Heads ... On Track

Remain In Light (1980)

Personnel:
David Byrne: lead vocals, keyboards, guitar, bass, percussion, vocal arrangements
Jerry Harrison: keyboards, guitar, percussion, backing vocals
Tina Weymouth: keyboards, bass, percussion, backing vocals
Chris Frantz: keyboards, drums, percussion, backing vocals
Brian Eno: keyboards, guitar, bass, percussion, backing vocals, vocal arrangements
Adrian Belew: guitar, Roland guitar synthesizer ('Crosseyed And Painless', 'The Great Curve', 'Listening Wind', 'The Overload')
Robert Palmer: percussion
José Rossy: percussion
Jon Hassell: horns
Nona Hendryx: backing vocals
Producer: Brian Eno
Recorded: July-August 1980
Studios: Compass Point, Nassau, Bahamas; Sigma Sound, New York City
Release date: 8 October 1980
Running time: 40:10
Label: Sire
Album charts: US: 19, UK: 21
Singles charts: 'Once In A Lifetime', UK 14; 'Houses In Motion', UK: 50

For a while, it seemed as though *Fear Of Music* might be the band's final album. In *This Must Be The Place*, David Bowman recounts a scene around this time when Weymouth pleaded with her husband to disengage from Byrne: 'Let's leave him! Let's do our own thing! We should have him kicked out of the band! We never needed him! We never needed him as much as he needs us!'

Talking Heads without David Byrne was a bad idea whose time had not yet come. (The 1996 album *sans* Byrne, *No Talking, Just Head*, would show just how ill-conceived the idea was.) However, it would take some work to keep the band together. Byrne and Eno were busy collaborating on an album titled *My Life In The Bush Of Ghosts* that pointedly excluded the rest of the band. Its release was postponed until 1981, perhaps partly due to the fact that – according to Frantz – Weymouth was eventually able to entice Eno and Byrne into joining the other three band members in jam sessions at the Long Island City loft. They began taping the results, with Frantz noting in *Remain In Love*, 'You could hear all kinds of interesting parts germinating, mutating and evolving. There was nothing commercial or predictable about these little jams, and as we listened back, you could see smiles of surprise coming over our faces. There was just no denying that Talking Heads still had a great chemistry going on and the beats were good. You could dance to it!'

Harrison notes in *The Band And Their Music*, 'We deliberately switched

45

instruments because sometimes people can come up with a naïve part that somebody else might not come up with. On some things, I started out playing drums with Chris playing synthesizer, and later we switched back. That works quite well as a way of getting away from the things you fall into, in addition to being fun'.

As early as the recording of 'I Zimbra' at the *Fear Of Music* sessions, Eno had introduced the band to Nigerian musician Fela Kuti's 1973 album *Afrodiasiac*. This record, like much of Kuti's music, is built on a memorable riff that is extended for many minutes. In 2017, Byrne told the Library of Congress:

We were listening to African pop music, such that was available, like Fela Kuti and King Sunny Adé, and some field recordings. But we didn't set out to imitate those. We deconstructed everything, and then, as the music evolved, we began to realize we were, in effect, reinventing the wheel. Our process led us to something with some affinity to afro-funk, but we got there the long way 'round, and, of course, our version sounded slightly off. We didn't get it quite right, but in missing, we ended up with something new.

In *How Music Works*, Byrne echoes Frantz's description of the band's song-making process, although Byrne presents it as a more formally structured endeavor:

We worked rapidly. One or two people would lay down a track, usually some kind of repetitive groove that would last about four minutes, the presumed length of a song. Maybe it would be a guitar riff or a drum part, or maybe a sequenced arpeggio pattern and an intermittent guitar squeal. Others would then respond to what had been put down, adding their own repetitive parts filling in the gaps and spaces for the whole length of the *song*. As we'd listen to one part being recorded, we'd all be scheming about what we could add. It was a kind of game.

A game it might have been, but it was a collaborative enterprise, with everyone's creativity being acknowledged. This way of working probably saved the band from breaking up, and it certainly led to a groundbreaking album when they headed back to Compass Point Studios in the Bahamas to piece everything together. Interestingly, while Talking Heads were recording *Remain In Light* in Studio A, a very different band was working on a very different masterpiece next door: in Studio B, rock band AC/DC were recording *Back In Black*.

Byrne said of the *Remain In Light* recording sessions, 'Only Adrian Belew and a couple of percussionists were added to the core band. The magic of multi-tracking meant we could add parts ourselves: Jerry could play a guitar part and then add a keyboard track later. We built up 24 tracks of knotty interwoven parts, and by switching groups of them on and off, we could create sections that might work in place of conventional verses and choruses'.

Once again, the lyrics were written after the music was recorded. In *The Band And Their Music*, Byrne acknowledged that on the group's first three albums, 'A lot of the song structures have me ranting and raving in a limited melodic range'. For *Remain In Light*, he drew much of his lyric inspiration from 'the evangelists one hears on the radio throughout the US ... In the more exciting preaching, I think they're going after a thing similar to the music. But I'm just not very direct about it. I like to plant just the seed of an idea in someone's head rather than telling him exactly what to think'.

The recording of Byrne's vocals didn't require the presence of the other band members, which 'felt hurtful' to Frantz and Weymouth, whom Eno asked to leave the control room at one point, even though between them, the pair were paying for half the studio time. In frustration, the couple turned to the creation of the album's now-iconic cover. The front has the band name at the top in large white letters on a strip of black, with two upside down 'A's that feel vaguely Cyrillic. The title is in a much smaller font at the bottom. Band member headshots in a blue wash take up the rest of the space. But, using then-new technology, Weymouth and Frantz digitally painted in red over all the faces, leaving only the hair, eyes, nose, and mouth of each musician showing.

On the back cover are four Grumann Avenger airplanes (the type piloted by Weymouth's father) flying over an alpine landscape. Though they are US Navy planes, they are digitally dyed red and have been given green stars on their wings and fuselages, so they appear to be Communist invaders or possibly representations of the four Talking Heads.

Despite, or perhaps because of, the band members' lively competing opinions, the end result was an album that's sometimes compared to The Beatles' *Sgt. Pepper's Lonely Hearts Club Band*, in as much as it expanded the group's earlier ideas and musicianship in a way that seemed to open entirely new doors for popular music. In fact, a better comparison might be to an album a couple of decades in the future: Radiohead's *Kid A*. Both *Fear Of Music* and Radiohead's *OK Computer* were third albums that seemed light years ahead of the records that preceded them but still made use of traditional hooks and musical structures. *Remain In Light* and *Kid A* blew those expectations apart.

Reviews, as always, were glowing. Ken Tucker wrote in *Rolling Stone*: 'On *Remain In Light*, rhythm takes over. Each of the eight compositions adheres to a single guitar/drum riff repeated endlessly, creating what funk musicians commonly refer to as a groove. A series of thin, shifting layers is then added – more jiggly percussion, glancing and contrasting guitar figures, singing by Byrne that represents a sharp and exhilarating break with the neurotic and intentionally wooden vocals that had previously characterized all Talking Heads albums'. Robert Christgau believed that this was the album 'in which

David Byrne conquers his fear of music in a visionary Afro-Funk synthesis: clear-eyed, detached, almost mystically optimistic'.

Retrospective reviews from decades after the album's release continued to find *Remain In Light* magical. Writing for the BBC, Mike Diver noted that the album 'illustrates how keen ambition could gel with commercial nous, with results that dazzle'. Barry Walsh argued in *Slant* that the album 'proves that Byrne and company truly had their fingers on the metronomic pulse of modern culture, mirroring it with their music, all the while casting a watchful eye ahead to where it could go next'. And Kenneth Partridge in *Billboard* praised a 'strangely brilliant album from a band that did strange and brilliant better than anyone'.

With all four members contributing to the music, naturally, they all wanted credit for all the songs. Initially, Byrne and Eno agreed, with the writing credits supposed to be going to all five. But when the record came out (at the insistence of Eno and Byrne, the others suspected), the credits actually read 'All songs written by David Byrne & Brian Eno (except 'Houses In Motion' and 'The Overload', written by David Byrne, Brian Eno and Jerry Harrison)'. The songwriting credits were later corrected for the CD release, but in a 2009 interview in *The Quietus*, Frantz said that he and his wife 'felt very burned'. The pair would, to varying degrees, continue to resent Byrne, but the music itself usually sounded buoyant, if not joyous. In 2000, Eno told NPR's David Karr, 'That record is terribly optimistic in a way. It's very up and looking *out* to the world and saying, 'What a fantastic place we live in. Let's celebrate it'. And I think we knew that was a fresh thought at the time'.

'Born Under Punches (The Heat Goes On)' (Lyrics: Byrne, Eno; Music: Byrne, Frantz, Harrison, Weymouth, Eno)
The opening track begins with a drum fill and an 'Ah!' from Byrne before launching into the groove it will stick with for the next five minutes and 45 seconds: staccato rhythm guitar, funky bass, African-inspired drumming, synthesizers swooping in and out with short, high-pitched notes that sound like a computer or a video game gone awry. As the band and countless critics have pointed out, the music closely resembles the sound achieved on 'I Zimbra': big and danceable, hook-laden yet mostly devoid of traditional chord changes.

Soon, the singer is asking us to take a look at his hands. He tells us, 'The hand speaks/The hand of a government man', and, of course, we think back to the singer of 'Don't Worry About The Government', who so admired civil servants and spent his time thinking about his favorite laws 'made in Washington, D.C'. But this persona is very different. He's 'a tumbler/Born under punches' and 'so thin'. The earlier character was satisfied with his work and his delightful building, but the persona here needs far less: 'All I want is to breathe'.

Variations on the opening verse conclude with what sounds like the singer talking to himself: 'Take a look at these hands/You don't have to mention it/ No thanks, I'm a government man'. An appropriately disjointed guitar solo signals the middle of the song. In a 2022 *Guitar Player* interview with Harrison and guitarist Adrian Belew, Harrison said, 'That's David. He's using a Lexicon Prime Time delay and working the hold button. You could record little bits and mess with how fast it played back. It was done piece by piece'.

The phrase 'Goes on, and the heat goes on' occurs 68 times. Even with the occasional interpolation of 'Where the hand has been', the sung words began to sound more like a chant, a rock 'n' roll version of the sacred syllable 'Om'. Before long, Byrne begins singing in counterpoint, doubled in a lower octave with a reverb effect, almost sounding like a small choir. Various phrases from the opening verses reappear, but most conspicuous are the lines 'All I want is to breathe/Won't you breathe with me?' In this new context, the singer sounds less psychotic and paranoid and more like someone who is simply, patiently pleading for connection with his fellow human beings.

'Crosseyed And Painless' (Lyrics: Byrne, Eno; Music: Byrne, Frantz, Harrison, Weymouth, Eno)
'Crosseyed And Painless' chugs right into motion with a minor chord guitar riff that continues to the fadeout. It's a danceable, upbeat rhythm accented with synths and guitar licks. Byrne enters with a now-familiar statement of dissociation and disenfranchisement: 'Lost my shape, trying to act casual/Can't stop/I might end up in the hospital/Changing my shape, I feel like an accident'. The chorus (eight repetitions of 'I'm still waiting') perfectly fits the music's static nature, as we realize there will be no significant tonal shifts from what was delivered in the opening seconds.

The midpoint offers listeners the first hint of what Adrian Belew's guitar playing will bring to the album. He's not a virtuoso in the manner of Jimi Hendrix or Frank Zappa, but his solos do make an impression. With more sonic landscaping rather than traditional scales, they are the perfect mood enhancer for the music's marriage of funk and paranoia.

Ken Tucker wrote in his *Rolling Stone* review that the music 'lurches about while always moving forward; thrust ahead by the tough, serene beat of the bass and percussion ... phrases are suggested and measured, repeated and turned inside out, in reaction to the spins and spirals of their organizing riff melodies'.

The second set of 'Crosseyed And Painless' lyrics finds the singer stranded on the 'island of doubt', clearly confused by what's going on around him. But soon, he zeroes in on the problem: facts. Similar to his extended critique in 'Animals', Bryne provides a long list of the problems with facts: 'Facts are lazy and facts are late/Facts don't come with points of view/Facts don't do what I want them to'. Byrne sings this litany in a comic, almost robotic voice, and it would be easy to write it off as the ravings of another of his paranoid characters. However, four years later, when the movie *Stop Making Sense* came out, we saw just how much fun he was having singing this song as the film's final, jubilant number.

'The Great Curve' (Lyrics: Byrne; Music: Byrne, Frantz, Harrison, Weymouth, Eno)

Musically, there is certainly a family resemblance between the album's first three songs. 'The Great Curve' is also lively, percussion-heavy and punctuated with rapid-fire bursts of rhythm guitar, with Jon Hassell's horns energizing the rhythm section. The lyric, however, is downright philosophical compared to some of the more quirky lyrics in the Byrne canon.

Initially, the title appears to refer to our own home orb, Earth: 'Sometimes the world has a load of questions/Seems like the world knows nothing at all'. But in verse two, we are introduced to a woman who 'is moving to describe the world'. Apparently, she is a prophetess, for 'She has messages for everyone' and the 'hands that guide her are invisible'. Alas, sinister forces seem to be at work because, after each line, Byrne sings about the woman, the chorus responds with 'Night must fall now! Darker! Darker!'

In *How Music Works*, Byrne says that this lyric was 'inspired by Robert Farris Thompson's writings about African spirituality, and the feminine goddess that survives today in remnants like Mother Nature or Yansan and Oshun in Afro-Atlantic cultures'. He concludes, 'I wasn't writing about my own anxieties anymore. I had to leave much of that behind'. It's an open question as to how well Byrne succeeded in capturing the world spirit, but it clearly felt like a breakthrough for him as a lyricist.

A little before two minutes in, Adrian Belew's guitar takes things in a different direction. Speaking to *Guitar Player* in 2022, Belew described how he came to make these sounds: 'I'm using my battered old Strat through a Roland Jazz Chorus 120. I had three or four pedals. I think it was a Big Muff and an equalizer that I used to boost the mid-range. Also, my Stratocaster had a Strat-O-Blaster that really upped the output. I had an Electric Mistress, too, so when it starts doing all the crazy, weird sounds, that's just me stepping on that and introducing it into the chain'. That technical description may resonate with guitarists, but it doesn't go very far toward describing the guttural gut-punch of the sound itself. 'Chunky', 'grunting', 'atavistic' and 'animalistic' are all apt adjectives that have been used to describe Belew's playing.

The solo lasts for 90 seconds before we return to the conjunction of the world and the 'She'. Now we learn that 'The world moves on a woman's hips/ The world moves and it swivels and bops'. Perhaps she is more than a prophet: she is an Earth mother, a goddess. Suddenly, hope surges into the lyrics: 'A world of light/She's gonna open our eyes up'. At first, the choral response continues its warning: 'Night must fall now! Darker! Darker!' But before long, there's a counter-response: 'Divine, to define/She is moving to define/So say so, so say so'. Then there are three vocal strands braiding back and forth, pausing long enough to emphasize the affirmative idea that 'She's gonna open our eyes up', before shifting back to the *mélange* of words that become hard to parse from one another.

The track feels like it's heading to a fade out when, with about a minute left, Belew returns with his groaning, growling, straining, aching, bellowing guitar, and the song finally fades on those tortured guitar notes, with many of the original listeners watching in wonder as the stylus moved towards the turntable's spindle before lifting-up into silence.

'Once In A Lifetime' (Lyrics: Byrne; Music: Byrne, Frantz, Harrison, Weymouth, Eno)
Side two starts with what became a signature Talking Heads song. Speaking to Rick Karr in a 2000 NPR piece on the song, Tina Weymouth recalled saying to Frantz, 'I went up and picked up the bass, and you were yelling in your corner, and I couldn't quite hear what you were saying. But you were yelling something at me, and you were saying, 'Bah *dah* bomp bomp. Bomp bomp bomp'. And as soon as I started doing that, you said, 'That's more like it!"

The lyric arrived by a different route. In Jim Bevigilia's book *Playing Back The '80s: A Decade Of Unstoppable Hits*, Frantz states: 'According to legend, and I believe it's true, (Byrne) rented a car and basically drove around the American South and listened to Pentecostal preachers on the radio. Fire and brimstone that you still hear on certain radio stations in the South, particularly on a Sunday morning. That type of preaching and messaging was the big inspiration for his lyrics on 'Once In A Lifetime'.' Byrne confirmed the essence of that story when talking to NPR's Karr: 'So much of it was taken from the style of radio evangelists. And so I would improvise lines as if I was giving a sermon in that kind of meter, in that kind of hyperventilating style, and then go back and distill that'.

After the now-famous bass riff, accompanied by a shimmering synthesizer, Byrne's imagination immediately kicks into high gear. Using the second-person perspective (unusual for him), he announces, 'You may find yourself behind the wheel of a large automobile/And you may find yourself in a beautiful house with a beautiful wife/And you may ask yourself, 'Well, how did I get here?" The lines are spoken, not sung, and if Byrne sounds vaguely like a Southern radio preacher, he sounds equally like himself, the guy who always sees the world at a canted angle. Byrne told Karr: 'We're largely unconscious. You know, we operate half awake or on autopilot, and end up, whatever, with a house and family and job and everything else, and we haven't really stopped to ask ourselves, 'How did I get here?"

The unsettled feeling Preacher Byrne seems to be trying to instill in his flock (echoing the poet Rilke, 'You must change your life!') is counterbalanced by the sung chorus, which seems to argue for a live-and-let-live approach to the world, one of 'Letting the days go by'. Granted, water is holding the speaker down, but he's not drowning in it. Indeed, there seems to be water *beneath* the water. 'There is water at the bottom of the ocean', he tells us redundantly, adding, 'Under the water, carry the water/Remove the water at the bottom of the ocean/Water dissolving and water removing'. It doesn't quite make sense, but the overall feeling is one of acceptance and letting go of *flow*. Thus, the tagline 'Same as it ever was', which could be read as a shrug of defeat ('Nothing ever changes'), can just as easily be heard as an affirmation, as though Byrne were saying, 'The world is as it is. Let it be'.

'Houses In Motion' (Lyrics: Byrne; Music: Byrne, Frantz, Harrison, Weymouth, Eno)

Three sampled notes introduce a mumbling spoken-word verse over perhaps the album's funkiest musical backing, with the guitars laid-back and grooving. You can just barely make out the hapless protagonist's complaints: 'For a long time I felt without style or grace/Wearing shoes with no socks in cold weather'. However, the speaker believes in himself – 'I knew my heart was in the right place' – which is confusing because, in the next verse, he's referring to someone in the third person who is 'digging his own grave'.

This hardly seems like a formula for the album's second single, but suddenly Byrne is singing with all his might, that he's 'walking a line', and the track really kicks into gear. The central motion of the song is the call-and-response of the chorus, with Byrne taking both parts of the conversation. 'Get outta the way', he sings in the high voice we know best. Then, as if answering himself, he responds in a lower tone, 'No time to begin', 'This isn't the time', the high voice argues, followed by the lower-pitched reply, 'So nothing was done'. Then the tenor 'I'm turning around' receives the baritone response, 'No trouble at all'. This schizophrenic motion drives everything forward, turning each line into its own hook, with the two voices combining at the end of the chorus.

In the next verse, we've left behind 'I' and 'he', and the focus is on a 'she' who 'has closed her eyes/She has give up hope'. The gesture of moving outside of traditional grammar with the final verb is unusual for Byrne. Is he trying to be *cool* (a posture for which he is ill-suited)? Is he quoting someone else? It's hard to tell when the subject matter is so open to interpretation. In the book *Once In A Lifetime*, Ian Gittins characterized the verses as 'sketchily drawn, ill-defined character pieces', a description that could apply to many Byrne songs up to that point.

A careless listener might at first mistake the instrumental after the second chorus as another Belew solo, but, in fact, it's horn player Jon Hassel offering a similarly unconventional response to the unconventional music. The anxiety woven into the lyric finds its wordless expression in what might be described as early 1970s Miles Davis blowing his impression of a dying elephant. The chorus returns and then Hassel has a final minute to take the song to its inconclusive conclusion, accompanied in the fade-out by the oddly happy-sounding keyboard.

Overall, 'Houses In Motion' has the feel of an Eno composition, perhaps something circa his album *Before And After Science*, though Hassell's contribution makes it feel like avant-garde jazz, and there are also hints of

King Sunny Adé and Funkadelic. However, none of these comparisons quite hit the mark: the song is, ultimately, just itself, a landmark in their catalog.

'Seen And Not Seen' (Lyrics: Byrne; Music: Byrne, Frantz, Harrison, Weymouth, Eno)
The album's shortest and probably weakest track consists of a spoken-word disquisition on the nature of identity. Using the faux-naïf voice Byrne was to adopt as the narrator in the film version of *True Stories*, he imagines a character ('he') who speculates whether people can change their faces by wishing for them to be different. As a half-developed story idea in an undergraduate creative-writing class, 'Seen And Not Seen' might be worth discussing, but as a spoken-word poem on what's purportedly one of the best albums of the decade, if not of all time, the piece falls awfully flat. Luckily, Byrne's voice is so low in the mix that it's sometimes difficult to hear what he's saying, so it's possible to pretend that the text is more profound or funnier than it actually is.

The music is pleasant enough. The usual funky rhythm is toned down, with flashes of synthesizer, guitar and vocalese swooping into the mix like swallows in the evening. With a sung lyric, this track might have been a standout. However, while Eno and Talking Heads generally knew what to leave in and what to toss out, this song is an exception.

'Listening Wind' (Lyrics: Byrne; Music: Byrne, Frantz, Harrison, Weymouth, Eno)
Acoustic percussion gives 'Listening Wind' the most purely African-inspired opening on *Remain In Light*. Then, 15 seconds in, kick drum, bass, and synthesizer return the album to its signature sonic landscape, with Belew's guitar effects adding mysterious notes in preparation for the vocal. Even more than in 'Seen And Unseen', Byrne's voice during the verses is buried in the mix, but the story he's speak-singing this time is very different. While Talking Heads' generally contrarian attitude might be called political, Byrne's lyrics are far more likely to ruminate on love than politics. That's not the case with 'Listening Wind'.

The protagonist is a man named Mojique. His nationality is unclear (a Google search of the name mostly returned references to a Japanese video game and 'Listening Wind' itself), but the era of the song's composition, along with the African and Arabian-sounding instrumentation, suggests an Islamic and/or North African country. Mojique is a terrorist, but he's presented in a flattering light. Yes, he sends bombs through the mail to Americans and plants explosive 'devices through the Free Trade Zone', but he is 'on a mission' for the greater good. In the 'days before Americans came', his homeland was a better place, and now 'He feels the power of the past behind him/He has the knowledge of the wind to guide him on'.

Like the water in 'Once In A Lifetime', the wind here has some negative connotations – it blows 'the dust' into Mojique's head, but it's primarily a factor for good. It is there to guide and comfort him as he goes about his work of trying to drive the Americans out of the 'streets and alleys' where he lives. His work is made more appealing by the lovely chorus. The simple lines 'The wind in my heart/The dust in my head' are accompanied by an equally simple movement between minor and major chords, and Byrne sings the lines with a straightforward sincerity that is absent from much of his work.

In a 2004 interview with Peter Ross in Glasgow's *The Herald*, Byrne was asked if he had any sympathy for 'people who are perpetrating acts of terror against the United States'. He replied, 'Yeah, I think I do a little bit. But you never know; I'm not there. I certainly understand a part of it. I understand why America is not universally loved. That's been obvious to me for years and years, but it's not obvious to a lot of Americans. Their immediate reaction is, 'They love us, they're just jealous. They just want McDonald's'.'

But Mojique doesn't want McDonalds. He wants revolution, and the song is frequently cited by listeners who feel Talking Heads' role as progressive activists has been undervalued.

'The Overload' (Lyrics: Byrne; Music: Byrne, Frantz, Harrison, Weymouth, Eno)
Listeners hoping for a rousing closing number on *Remain In Light* will be disappointed. Granted, with the exception of 'Houses In Motion', the songs on side two are generally less energetic, but 'The Overload' is downright lugubrious.

In *The Band And Their Music*, Byrne says the song 'was influenced by things I'd *read* about Joy Division ... and it was an exciting idea to me ... When I finally heard them, I was disappointed. They sounded closer to a rock group than I thought they were'. The notion of a rock song that's not a rock song clearly informs 'The Overload', which begins with synthesizer, Adrian Belew's guitar notes, a doleful three-note bass line and Frantz's least energetic drumming on the album. Before Byrne's vocal kicks in, the song could easily be mistaken for the intro to something long and complicated by King Crimson.

Up to this point, when Byrne has been singing, he's been able to create melodies atop a single chord, but 'The Overload' settles in as an echoey dirge. The lyric mirrors the music. We learn that 'A terrible signal/Too weak to even recognize' has caused 'A gentle collapsing/The removal of the insides'. Admittedly, there is a kind of resigned wisdom in the words. Byrne acknowledges that 'We're older than we realize/In someone's eyes' and that a 'gentle collapsing' is occurring on 'every surface' of 'the quiet road' he and his partner(s) travel. Meanwhile, Belew's guitar whines and moans at a meandering half-speed between and during the singing ('It was so improvised', he told *Guitar Player* magazine).

While many listeners believed 'The Overload' achieved a kind of quiet, benedictory dignity, Ken Tucker of *Rolling Stone* felt the song was a 'droning drag, full of screeching guitar noise that's more freaked-out than felt'. Regardless of its merits, or lack thereof, the track feels every second of its six-minute length.

Talking Heads ... *On Track*

The Name Of This Band Is Talking Heads (Live) (1982)

Personnel:
David Byrne: guitar, vocals
Chris Frantz: drums
Tina Weymouth: bass, synthesizer, percussion, backing vocals
Jerry Harrison: guitar, piano, keyboards, synthesizer, backing vocals
Adrian Belew: guitar, backing vocals
Nona Hendryx: backing vocals ('Life During Wartime', 'Take Me To The River', 'The Great Curve')
Busta 'Cherry' Jones: additional bass
Dolette McDonald: percussion, backing vocals
Steve Scales: congas, percussion
Bernie Worrell: keyboards, backing vocals
Producer: Talking Heads
Recorded: 17 November 1977, Maynard, Massachusetts; 17 November 1979, Passaic, New Jersey; 27 August 1980, New York; 8-9 November 1980, Cherry Hill, New Jersey
Release date: 24 March 1982
Running time: 81:37 (LP); 156:30 (expanded CD)
Labels: Sire, Rhino (reissue)
Album charts: US: 32, UK: 22

While Robert Christgau gave *The Name Of This Band Is Talking Heads* an A- grade, he said, 'Live albums by essentially non-improvisatory artists who do definitive work in the studio are always slightly extraneous'. That's not *quite* right. Talking Heads was a superb live band, and their two live albums (this one and *Stop Making Sense*), released in 1982 and 1984, respectively, provide a sense of the energy and excitement the band brought to the stage. Nevertheless, the songs, as Christgau suggests, mostly hew to the outlines of the recorded versions. Unlike, say, Yes's *Yessongs* – where a three-and-a-half-minute number such as 'Long Distance Runaround' is given a nearly 14-minute treatment – *The Name Of This Band Is Talking Heads* may showcase a slightly longer solo or an extra chorus or two, but even the extended, crowd-pleasing 'Take Me To The River' mostly depends on repetition for its length.

Still, to give the live band the props it deserves, I will make a few remarks about each of the songs as they appeared on the original live LPs. (The expanded CD remasters of Talking Heads' two live albums are nearly twice as long as the original issues, and I won't be covering that bonus material because it rarely offers significant variations on the definitive studio versions of the songs.)

Two tracks appear on *The Name Of This Band Is Talking Heads* that had not appeared on the first four studio albums. 'Building On Fire', originally

56

titled 'Love → Building On Fire', their first single, is discussed in the chapter 'Studio Songs Not Included on the Original Studio Albums' at the end of the book. 'A Clean Break (Let's Work)' was something altogether new for those who hadn't attended Talking Heads concerts, and it will receive a longer analysis in this section.

Released in March 1982, the first live album was meant to fill a gap. 1982 was the first calendar year without a new Talking Heads studio album since their first record. (More about the reasons for that interruption will be discussed in the next chapter.) Side one – the first five songs – comes from a live studio broadcast on 17 November 1977, one month after the release of *Talking Heads: 77*. The recording was made at radio station WCOZ (now WJMN) in Maynard, Massachusetts, which broadcast to the greater Boston area. Side two – the second five songs – was recorded at the Capitol Theater in Passaic, New Jersey, on the same date in 1979, ten weeks after *Fear Of Music* was released, though only 'Air' and 'Memories Can't Wait' were played from that album. The recordings are crisp and the band is *on*. Yet what these tracks mostly prove is that Talking Heads did a good job of reproducing their early songs on stage.

The second disc of the two-LP set focuses on albums three and four. The songs on sides three ('I Zimbra' through 'Life During Wartime') and four (the final three songs) were recorded at a concert in Central Park on 27 August 1990 and at Emerald City nightclub in Cherry Hill, New Jersey, on 8 and 9 November 1990. As noted below, despite the fact that the performing band, including backing singers, had doubled in size, these recordings were less successful at capturing the Eno-produced sound of *Fear Of Music* and *Remain In Light*. That remarkable feat would have to wait for *Stop Making Sense*.

It's not just that the studio magic is missing on the second record. In *The Band And Their Music*, Weymouth addresses the elephant in the room. When acclaimed bassist Busta 'Cherry' Jones was in the group, 'it was a lot of fun, but it was also like two kings in one palace. It just didn't work out that well. When King Sunny Adé came to this country, he had seven drummers and five guitar players, but there was still only one bass player'. As a result of Byrne's decision to add Jones to the band, Weymouth gave Busta 'more of my parts and invented new ones for myself to play, either on keyboards or guitar, or just to sing, which was something I hadn't attempted in the group before'.

On sides three and four, Talking Heads are not the same band, in fact, or in spirit. You can see it in the 1980 concert in Rome (available on YouTube), where Weymouth, Frantz and Harrison are doing their best to look happy but are clearly outshone by the musicians who are not official group members. Busta Jones and Adrian Belew bop around the stage, percussionist Steve Scales has a lot more energy and presence than Frantz, and Dolette McDonald sings better than anyone up there, including Byrne.

The front and back of the album cover reflect the two eras the LPs were recorded in, and they emphasize just how much the band had changed in a few years. The nine photographs on the front cover show the band in the New Jersey loft with the ruffled curtains and orange carpet that critic David Bowman found so 'awful'. They look stiff and amateurish (Who plays a gig in a living room?) and, above all, very young. On the back cover, they are on stage at an arena, with professional lighting and backing musicians dressed in cool clothes: all rock stars, for sure.

The four original members managed to work through the contradictions and complications of this Byrne-inspired lineup on their next studio album, *Speaking In Tongues*. And Jonathan Demme mostly did a good job of disguising any group tensions in the film version of *Stop Making Sense*, by which time Busta Jones had departed. However, the music on the first live album's second disc represents something of a conundrum. We can't help but wonder who 'This' refers to in the album title.

'New Feeling' (Byrne)

'The name of this song is 'New Feeling'', Byrne announces at the beginning of the album. 'That's what it's about'. Then, as Frantz smashes the hi-hat and Byrne plays the introductory riff on guitar, it sounds almost as though you are there, sitting a few feet away from the band in the studio of a radio station. Each instrument is distinct. Byrne and Harrison's guitar parts blend well over Weymouth's confident and quietly inventive bass. Above all, Frantz's drumming is as steady as one of the good friends Byrne is always talking about.

'A Clean Break (Let's Work)' (Byrne)

After a smattering of small-audience applause, the band kick in with a punky vibe led by the two electric guitars. After repeating the line 'Just beginning to take that love away', Byrne's shrill voice erupts into a shout: 'In a minute, I'll wash that love away'. The verse lyric illustrates another of the Byrnian paradoxes associated with thwarted love. 'We'd be together if we cut that love away', he sings, seeming to imply that if he and his beloved were not in love, they would be able to have a relationship.

The pre-chorus builds tension over lines like 'It's a matter of degrees/And that's true', then the chorus kicks in, with Byrne warbling, 'Take that love away' four times. Amazingly, it sounds – just for the chorus – like an actual love song, especially when he holds the final note at the end of the fourth line.

But, of course, true love has no place in the music of 1977-era Talking Heads, and the post-chorus section, despite using the chorus chords, undercuts everything with shouted protests of nonsense syllables, which we know well signal Byrne's anxiety, or his refusal to take something seriously, or both.

The middle solo finds the two guitarists firing back and forth, with bass in the middle, getting funky and holding it all together. The track's final third repeats everything but verse two, with Byrne's singing becoming more sardonic and unhinged. The chorus provides a welcome respite of melody, and then, after the gibberish, it's all over.

At almost five minutes in length, 'A Clean Break' is on the long-ish side for early Talking Heads, but it was a song they often played in early concerts, and it might well have made the cut for *Talking Heads: 77*. It's certainly a worthwhile addition to their catalog, and it's a shame that (at the moment) it can only be found on this album.

'Don't Worry About The Government' (Byrne)

Byrne lets out a rare laugh when announcing, 'The name of this song is 'Don't Worry About The Government'. It's a decent version of one of their best songs, though Harrison's keyboard-playing feels a bit stiff, and Byrne's singing is sometimes exaggerated, possibly a way to compensate for nerves. It's fun to hear him really stretching out the final note, which he holds for six seconds, but the rendition on *Talking Heads: 77* is clearly superior.

'Pulled Up' (Byrne)

This is one of their earlier numbers, and they know it well, delivering an exciting version. The two guitars, bass and drums blend seamlessly. And for all the inherent sarcasm ('Mommy, Daddy, come and look at me now'), the song feels optimistic and uplifting. It may not have the production values of the studio version, but this 'Pulled Up' is a keeper.

'Psycho Killer' (Byrne, Frantz, Weymouth)

Side one ends, fittingly, with one of their signature songs, the last track from *Talking Heads: 77* on this album. The introduction is lengthened with some guitar work, but the familiar bass line anchors the number into the famous opening verse: 'I can't seem to face up to the facts/I'm tense and nervous and I can't relax'. Verse two surprises us with some alternative lyrics for the first three lines:

> I passed out hours ago
> I'm sadder than you'll ever know
> I close my eyes on this sunny day

The lyric in the studio version is more aggressive ('You're talking a lot/But you're not saying anything') and seems more in keeping with a psycho killer's persona, but it's interesting to hear where the song might have gone. The long outro, punctuated by blasts of distorted guitar, is a nice touch and is possibly an improvement on the original.

'Artists Only' (Byrne, Zieve)

Side two commences with Byrne calling out 'Here we go', and we have our first opportunity to hear how an Eno-produced song (from *More Songs About*

Buildings And Food) sounds without Eno's assistance. Pretty good, as it turns out. As we noted earlier, the second album consisted almost entirely of songs the band had been playing since before their first album, so 'Artists Only' is performed with panache. With its short, repetitive and slightly comic lyric adapted from Wayne Zieve's college manifesto, it's practically an instrumental, focusing on guitar and keyboards, and for a moment, it's almost possible to imagine the band as a nascent prog-rock project.

'Stay Hungry' (Byrne, Frantz)
Another *More Songs* track, 'Stay Hungry', like 'Artists Only', relies on musical savvy to counterbalance its repetitive lyric. Byrne plays an actual guitar solo with Harrison backing him on Rick Wakeman-esque keys. Again, there's the feel of progressive rock in the air, or at the very least, a desire to experiment with becoming a jam band. The artists make it almost to the end, but Byrne takes us back to punk rock with his closing snarl, 'Here I *am*'.

'Air' (Byrne)
'Hello?' Weymouth's faint voice calls into the microphone in preparation for singing backing vocals. The first *Fear Of Music* song on this live album feels like it needs something more than synthesizer to achieve the haunting sound of the original. Indeed, you can understand how Byrne might have convinced his bandmates to bring in additional musicians the following year. Weymouth is no Dolette McDonald in the singing department, and Byrne does the song no favors with his cartoon-character voices. That said, the chorus manages to capture some of the lovely eeriness heard on *Fear Of Music*. And it would be a shame to have never heard Byrne scoff, 'Some people don't know shit about the air!'

'Building On Fire' (Byrne)
Previously known as 'Love → Building On Fire', this track still sounds strong, even without the horns that drove the second half of the original version. (See 'Studio Songs Not Included On The Original Studio Albums' below.) Another number that they'd been playing in concert for years, this song – with its cryptic chorus, 'It's not love/Which is my face/Which is a building/Which is on fire' – counter-compensates for the lack of horns by returning in the second half to the muted instrumentation of the first half, although the bass will not be denied. After the second chorus, guitar with reverb takes us almost to the end of a more-than-satisfactory rendition.

'Memories (Can't Wait)' (Byrne, Harrison)
The final song on the first record demonstrates that aggressive guitars, a rumbling bass and a kickass drummer can drive just about any song over the finish line. A chorus effect on guitar helps to replicate some of the Eno wizardry from *Fear Of Music*, but mostly, Talking Heads have turned this

song into a loud mid-tempo rocker. And while much is lost in the way of nuance, their committed performance allows them to pull it off.

'I Zimbra' (Byrne, Eno, Ball)
A percussion-heavy beginning is followed by dense guitar parts played by Byrne, Harrison, Belew and Weymouth, who has been replaced on bass by Busta Jones. The verse vocals are truly a joint effort, with Belew and Dolette McDonald singing just as loudly as Byrne. Former Parliament-Funkadelic keyboardist Bernie Worrell's synthesizer doesn't quite reproduce the sound as heard on *Fear Of Music*, and while there's certainly a lot of energy in the performance, the sound is thinner and less appealing.

'Drugs' (Byrne, Eno)
Again, the technical skills of Eno's engineers are missed. Live, 'Drugs' relies on odd sounds from synthesizer and Belew's effects-laden guitar. Frantz on drums and Jones on bass keep the zigzag rhythm going, but poor Weymouth is stuck on keyboards again, drowned out by Worrell and Harrison. Steve Sacks's percussion always helps a song, and Belew's outro solo has the excitement one expects from a lead guitarist in front of a crowd. But Byrne's tendency to make snorting noises doesn't help the song at all.

'Houses In Motion' (Lyrics: Byrne; Music: Byrne, Frantz, Harrison, Weymouth, Eno)
By the time of the 1983 tour that was captured in *Stop Making Sense*, the expanded band had figured out how to capture some of the depth and presence of the songs from *Remain In Light*. But on *The Name of This Band Is Talking Heads*, they were still working out the kinks. Jones' bass is the centerpiece of this song, with Belew's extended solos accenting and arguing with the lyric. One element that *does* work better here is having the backing singers (McDonald and Weymouth) respond to Byrne's lines ('I'm turning around', 'No trouble at all', etc.) instead of having him essentially sing to himself. The final minute or so settles into a funky groove, though it is perhaps too long if you are not out on the dance floor.

'Life During Wartime' (Byrne, Frantz, Harrison, Weymouth)
The forward motion of the rhythm guitars and Byrne's rapid delivery of his memorable lyric keeps the focus on the post-apocalyptic story and makes this version a credible approximation of the original. The backing vocals of McDonald and Nona Hendryx add a splash of excitement, and it's nice to have Weymouth back on bass, demonstrating that she's just as capable a musician as Jones. Still, other than providing us with the song's final lines (which are lost in the fade-out on *Fear Of Music*), there's nothing much this live version does that the studio version didn't do as well or better.

'The Great Curve' (Lyrics: Byrne; Music: Byrne, Frantz, Harrison, Weymouth, Eno)

Not surprisingly, considering that both Weymouth and Jones play bass, 'The Great Curve' has a striking bottom end. The three guitarists – Byrne, Harrison, and Belew – keep the rhythm tight and driving while the lead vocal is joined and sometimes overcome by a full-throated backing ensemble consisting primarily of McDonald and Hendryx but accompanied by Belew and Worrell. For an early attempt to tackle a *Remain In Light* track live, this works pretty well. As in the original, it's primarily a conversation between the positive ('Divine, to define, she is moving to define') and the negative ('Night must fall now! Darker! Darker!'). And as on the live version of 'Houses In Motion', Belew has a bit more freedom with his solo, though there's nothing revelatory about this version of 'The Great Curve'.

'Crosseyed And Painless' (Lyrics: Byrne, Eno; Music: Byrne, Frantz, Harrison, Weymouth, Eno)

Aside from a few moments, Jones' bass line – like Weymouth's original – is fairly simple, so it's sad to see her relegated again to second keyboard and backing vocals. Belew's guitar solo is more intrusive than on *Remain In Light*, which, depending on how you like your rock gods, is either a good or bad thing. What's certain is that he loved to shred. If anything, this live version reveals just how monotonous the music is, cool guitar and puzzling lyrics notwithstanding.

'Take Me To The River' (Green, Hodges)

The most notable advantage of this version is the appearance of actual soul singers. McDonald and Hendryx frequently steal the show, though Byrne's vocal nearly rises to the challenge they present him with. Both Weymouth and Jones play bass, which feels redundant. At nearly six and a half minutes in length, the song was probably more fun to see live than to listen to on the recording, but it does make for a jubilant album closer.

Speaking In Tongues (1983)

Personnel:
David Byrne: vocals, guitar, keyboards, synthesizer, bass, percussion
Jerry Harrison: keyboards, synthesizer, guitar, backing vocals
Tina Weymouth: bass, backing vocals, synthesizer, guitar
Chris Frantz: drums, backing vocals, synthesizer
Wally Badarou: synthesizer ('Burning Down The House', 'Swamp', 'This Must Be The Place (Naive Melody)')
Bernie Worrell: synthesizer ('Girlfriend Is Better')
Alex Weir: guitar ('Making Flippy Floppy', 'Swamp', 'Moon Rocks', 'Pull Up The Roots')
Steve Scales: percussion ('Burning Down The House', 'Moon Rocks')
Raphael Dejesus: percussion ('Slippery People', 'I Get Wild/Wild Gravity', 'Pull Up The Roots')
David Van Tieghem: percussion ('I Get Wild/Wild Gravity', 'This Must Be The Place (Naive Melody)')
L. Shankar: double violin ('Making Flippy Floppy')
Richard Landry: saxophone ('Slippery People')
Nona Hendryx: backing vocals ('Slippery People')
Dolette McDonald: backing vocals ('Slippery People')
Producer: Talking Heads
Studios: Blank Tape, New York City; Sigma Sound, New York City; Compass Point, Nassau, Bahamas
Release date: 1 June 1983
Running time: 40:51 (LP); 46:56 (cassette)
Label: Sire
Album charts: US: 15, UK: 21
Singles charts: 'Burning Down The House', US: 9; 'This Must Be The Place (Naive Melody)', US: 62, UK: 51

In a promotional spot recorded at the time of the record's release, Byrne – deadpan, with his tongue at least partly in his cheek – introduced *Speaking In Tongues*:

> Hi, my name is David Byrne. I'm with the band Talking Heads. We have a new record, which should be out just about now, called *Speaking In Tongues*. It's strictly pop songs. I've made a conscious effort to write some songs that it's actually possible to sort of sing along with at some points, which I think might have been kind of difficult with some of our earlier material. Some of our earlier stuff, I think you could do that, but a lot of it I tended to screech. That was my singing style. So I tried to sing a little bit more because I do enjoy singing. And I thought I should give myself a chance to sing somewhere outside the shower.

It's classic Byrnian rhetoric – offhandedly funny and self-deprecating, yes, but his first-person singular claim to have written the songs ignores the fact that all band members were involved in the creation of the music, even if Byrne is the sole author of the lyrics. Weymouth and Frantz would not have been amused. Still, the fact that Byrne was pitching a new Talking Heads album means that interpersonal relations had not yet completely fallen apart. Nevertheless, one might well wonder what happened in the three years since the release of *Remain In Light*.

Most importantly, perhaps, with the stopgap release of *The Name Of This Band Is Talking Heads*, they were able to take some time off from one another. Frantz and Weymouth formed a band called the Tom Tom Club, whose eponymous first album went platinum, with its Weymouth-sung single, 'Genius of Love' reaching 31 in the US. Thanks also to the song 'Wordy Rappinghood', their music had become a staple of dance floors everywhere. Harrison's solo album *The Red And The Black* had not done nearly as well. But like Frantz and Weymouth, he had taken his own turn in the spotlight. In 1981, Byrne and Eno's collaboration *My Life In The Bush Of Ghosts* came out, and Byrne released his first solo album, *The Catherine Wheel*, written for choreographer Twyla Tharp's dance project. Both were critical darlings, though neither approached the popularity of Talking Heads' recordings.

The biggest change by far was that Brian Eno was gone. In a 1981 interview with the British magazine *The Face*, Weymouth expressed her discontent with the Byrne/Eno relationship: 'They're like two 14-year-old boys making an impression on each other. By the time they finished working together for three months, they were dressing like one another ... I can see them when they're 80 years old and all alone – There'll be David Bowie, David Byrne and Brian Eno, and they'll just talk to each other'.

In the 'Most Asked Questions' section in the *Popular Favorites 1976-1992* compilation liner notes, Byrne responds to the question 'What was Eno like?': 'He has a sense of adventure and humor ... was great to work with until the others and I sensed him wanting us to be his back-up band, his source for ideas. But he wasn't really *writing* the stuff. Okay, enough'.

As for Eno's absence when the band took over production and left the controls to engineer Butch Jones, Frantz writes in *Remain In Love*: 'We all agreed that, unfortunately, working with Brian Eno was no longer an option. He had simply become too demanding. For example, he would only fly on the Concorde, and expected us to pay for it. Brian had done a lot for Talking Heads, but Talking Heads had done even more for Brian Eno and his reputation as a producer'.

Frantz describes the musical process for *Speaking In Tongues* as a group effort, with the band jamming, often on different instruments and using the results (recorded on a boombox in either Frantz or Byrne's loft) as the starting point for actual songs. Frantz suggests that early on, this process was not an easy one because of Harrison's drinking: 'Tina and I were worried

Above: Talking Heads – from L-R: Chris Frantz, Jerry Harrison, Tina Weymouth, David Byrne – in 1988, the year of their final album, *Naked*. (*Alamy*)

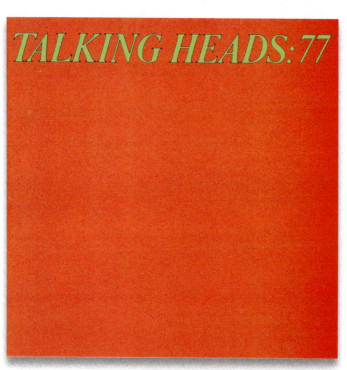

Left: The front cover of the band's first album (1977) with a design based on an idea by Byrne. (*Sire Records*)

Right: The cover of *More Song About Buildings And Food* (1978) features Polaroid photographs taken by Weymouth and Byrne based on work by Andrea Kovac. (*Sire Records*)

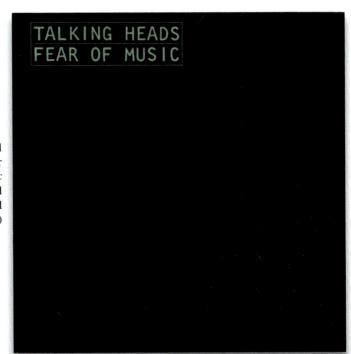

Right: The industrial metal flooring cover for *Fear Of Music* (1979) was designed by Harrison and Byrne. (*Sire Records*)

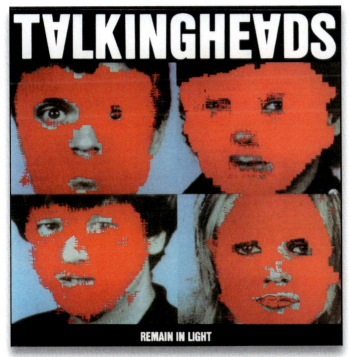

Left: Weymouth and Frantz conceived the *Remain In Light* (1980) front cover with help from MIT researcher Walter Bender. (*Sire Records*)

Above: A promo shot of the band in Amsterdam in 1976. From L-R: Frantz, Weymouth, Byrne and Harrison. (*Alamy*)

Below: The group performing at Entermedia Theater in Manhattan's East Village, circa 1977. (*Ebet Roberts/Getty Images*)

Right: Harrison and Byrne performing 'Psycho Killer' on the BBC 2 programme *The Old Grey Whistle Test*, January 1978.

Left: Harrison, Byrne and Weymouth, *OGWT*, 1978.

Right: The recently married Frantz and Weymouth, the band's rocking rhythm section, on *OGWT*, 1978.

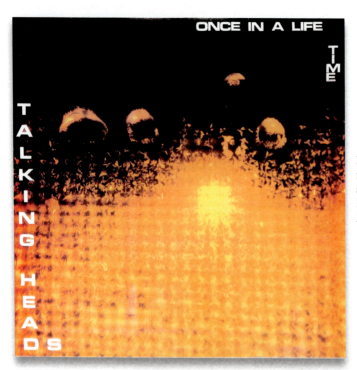

Left: The 45 rpm record cover for the single 'Once In A Lifetime' (1980). (*Sire Records*)

Right: The 45 rpm record cover for the single 'This Must Be The Place (Naive Melody)' (1983). (*Sire Records*)

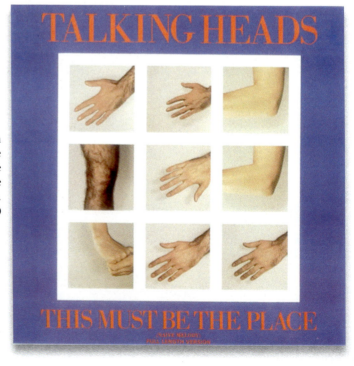

Right: The cover of *The Name Of This Band Is Talking Heads* (1982) shows the band playing in a living room in New Jersey in 1977. (*Sire Records*)

Left: The front cover of *Speaking In Tongues* (1983) was designed by Byrne. (*Sire Records*)

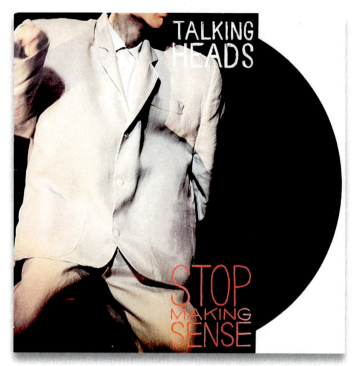

Left: Using a photo by Adele Lutz, the *Stop Making Sense* (1984) cover was designed by Byrne with Michael Hodgson and Jeffrey Ayeroff. (*Sire Records*)

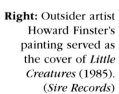

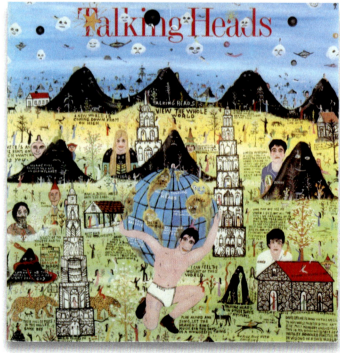

Right: Outsider artist Howard Finster's painting served as the cover of *Little Creatures* (1985). (*Sire Records*)

Right: The iconic cover of *True Stories* (1986) was designed by Michael Hodgson and Jeffrey Ayeroff using a logo by Bridget DeSoccio. (*Sire Records*)

Left: Paula Wright's portrait of a chimpanzee holding a violet in an elaborate frame adorns the cover of *Naked* (1988). (*Sire Records*)

Left: A still from the music video for 'And She Was' (1985), directed by avant-garde filmmaker Jim Blashfield, showing Weymouth and Frantz. (*Sire Records*)

Right: Another still from the 'And She Was' (1985) music video showing Byrne. (*Sire Records*)

Left: A still from the 'Road To Nowhere' (1985) music video, directed by Byrne and Stephen R. Johnson. (*Sire Records*)

Right: A still from the 'Love For Sale' (1986) music video, directed by Byrne and Melvin Sokolsky, with each band member assigned a color (Byrne's was yellow). (*Sire Records*)

Left: A still from the in-your-face music video for 'Blind' (1988), directed by Tibor Kalman and Sandy MacLeod. (*Sire Records*)

Right: A still from the 'Wild Wild Life (1986) music video, directed by Byrne, which included footage from his film *True Stories* (1986). (*Sire Records*)

Above: A promotional shot of Talking Heads in Bologna, Italy, 1982. (*Luciano Viti/Getty Images*)

Below: The band played dress up for the *Little Creatures* back cover image, captured by photographer Neil Selkirk. (*Sire Records*)

Above: A portrait of Talking Heads' lineup for the concert film *Stop Making Sense* (1984). From L-R: Steve Scales, Bernie Worrell, Harrison, Ednah Holt, Byrne, Lynn Mabry, Weymouth, Frantz and Alex Weir. (*Sire Records /Michael Ochs Archives/Getty Images*)

Below: The band performing in Belgrade, Yugoslavia, in 1982. From L-R: Weymouth, Frantz, Byrne, Scales, Weir. (*Brian Rasic/Getty Images*)

Left: A still of the band performing 'Burning Down The House' from *Stop Making Sense* (1984), directed by Jonathan Demme. From L-R: Byrne, Frantz, Weymouth, Weir.

Right: Holt, Mabry and Harrison grooving to the vibe of 'Burning Down The House'.

Left: The band in full throat on 'Burning Down The House'. From L-R: Holt, Mabry, Harrison, Byrne.

Right: A still from 'This Must Be The Place' from *Stop Making Sense*. From L-R: Weymouth, Holt, Mabry, Byrne, Frantz (in the background), Weir.

Left: Weymouth sneaking a smile at Byrne during 'This Must Be the Place'.

Right: Byrne dancing with the floor lamp during 'This Must Be The Place'.

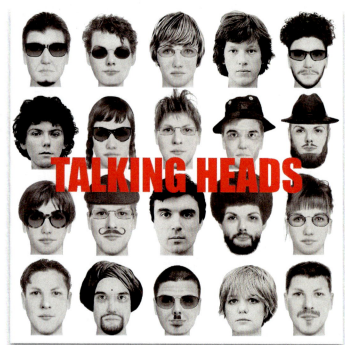

Left: The front cover of the compilation album *Popular Favorites 1976-1992: Sand In The Vaseline* (1992), painted by Byrne's famous friend Ed Ruscha. (*Sire/Warner Bros. Records*)

Right: The front cover of *The Best Of Talking Heads* (2004), with art direction and design by Hugh Brown using FACES facial composite software. (*Sire/Warner Bros. Records/Rhino Records*)

about Jerry. David, never much of a people person, said, 'We should kick him out of the band'.' However, Harrison cleaned up, and according to Frantz, 'The basic tracks were recorded quickly and almost effortlessly'. Indeed, the sound of the album is seamless, with every song displaying a strong family resemblance.

The recording process back at Compass Point in Nassau was amazingly similar to that of *Remain In Light*. But the inter-band tensions following the release of that album were largely absent from *Speaking In Tongues*, perhaps due to Eno's absence. In fact, even with the addition of a number of session musicians, Frantz said in *The Band And Their Music* that the making of the album 'was the easiest, most agreeable experience I've ever had with Talking Heads'.

In 1983, when Belgian television interviewer Annik Honoré asked Byrne why he called the album *Speaking In Tongues*, he replied, 'Well, I like the phrase, and because to me the lyrics have that kind of quality of not making logical sense, almost being a language of their own'. As many critics pointed out, the word-salad element of Byrne's writing was hardly new.

What *was* new this time was the inordinate amount of attention Byrne paid to a special version of the album cover. The one most people know was designed by him in conjunction with Tibor Carlman and shows photos of four upended chairs (in green, pink, blue, and violet) in each corner of the cover, with a blue spiral about the size of a 45rpm single in the center. The back cover, painted by Byrne, contains information about the album in the four corners, with a green, red, yellow, and blue color wheel in the center.

However, the cover Byrne preferred was far more elaborate. He'd struck up a friendship with artist Robert Rauschenberg, and Byrne encouraged his friend to design a deluxe edition of the record, which he hoped would only cost slightly more than the mass-produced cover. As Abigail Cain noted in a 2016 piece for *Artsy*, 'Rauschenberg referenced the three-color printing process by creating separate layers of cyan, magenta, and yellow. Each disc sported a collage, including a wrecked car, a highway billboard and a suburban bedroom, that could be spun to produce different effects'. Viewing the whole can be disorienting because, as Byrne pointed out, 'One could never see the full-color images at the same time, as Bob had perversely scrambled the separation'. Full-scale production of the Rauschenberg cover proved to be too expensive, though 50,000 copies were ultimately printed, and Rauschenberg won the 1984 Grammy Award for Best Album Design.

Talking Heads now expected their albums to garner elaborate critical praise, and this one was no exception. David Fricke raved in *Rolling Stone*: 'The Heads have never cut funk into finer, more fluent pieces. Nor have they ever displayed such a sense of purpose and playfulness'. *Time* magazine listed the album as one of the best of 1983, opining 'Soho soul and uptown rhythm: nobody mixes it up better'. No less a pillar of the establishment than the *Wall Street Journal* praised the 'renewed joy' that the band seemed to find in playing together. Of course, it's the critic's job to quibble, and while the ever-contrarian Robert Christgau gave the album an A- in *The Village Voice*, he couldn't refrain from some carping: 'Though God knows there's no rock-and-roll rule that says playfulness can't signify all by itself, the disjointed opacity of the lyrics fails to conceal Byrne's confusion about what it all means'. Byrne would likely have been more than willing to admit that confusion, but with their first million-selling album, there was no question that Talking Heads were once again on a roll.

'Burning Down The House' (Lyrics: Byrne; Music: Byrne, Frantz, Harrison, Weymouth)

In a 2023 *Fresh Air* interview with Terry Gross, Byrne explained the origin of the title of Talking Heads' biggest hit: 'The phrase 'burning down the house' I'd heard being used as a chant at a Parliament-Funkadelic concert that I'd seen. They didn't have it in a song. It was just a kind of chant that they started chanting, and the audience joined in and it meant, like, 'We're going to blow the roof off the sucker. We're going to set this place on fire. We're going to have a really amazing time here'. It didn't mean literally let's set fire to our houses or anything else. And the rest of it, I thought, let me see if I can make a song that is basically a lot of non-sequiturs that have a kind of emotional impact'.

In the liner notes of *Once In A Lifetime: The Best Of Talking Heads*, Weymouth tells the story differently, saying it was Frantz who'd been to the Parliament-Funkadelic concert, not Byrne. According to Weymouth, the singer had once again appropriated someone else's story as his own.

However the title came to be, it was certainly catchy, and for a while in the summer of 1983, in the midst of Ronald Reagan's first term as US President, the song was everywhere, on MTV and on the radio, peaking at nine on the *Billboard* Hot 100.

'Burning Down The House' offers listeners their first opportunity since *Talking Heads: 77* to hear the band without Eno's production, and nothing seems to have been lost with his departure. The song fades in on an acoustic guitar riff that's joined by three notes on synthesizer, the last note pitch-bent as it dies. The three notes repeat, with a single drum beat accompanying the final note. A drum fill and Byrne's 'Ahhh', and the song is off, synth bass up front, and plenty of voices amplifying certain initial phrases: 'Watch out!' 'Cool, babies!' 'Burning down the house!'

While the singer, as in most Byrne songs, is the central figure, he actually seems to be addressing people outside his immediate circle. 'Hold tight/We're in for nasty weather', he warns, and the phrase 'Fighting fire with fire' seems to imply that action will be taken by a group of people rather than one person alone. In a 1984 interview with NPR, Byrne stated that while he initially wasn't sure of the symbolic meaning of the burning house, after the album's release, he came to see it in psychological and mythological terms: 'It kind of implies ecstatic rebirth, or transcending one's own self. Like in classic psychology, the house is the self. Then burning it down is destroying yourself, and the assumption is that you get reborn, like a phoenix from the ashes'.

Wally Badarou's solo (punctuated by overdubbed tom fills) is all synthesizer, chunky and groovy, something like an Adrian Belew jam, but less aggressive, more radio-friendly. After two more verses, at 2:50 – the traditional endpoint for a hit single in the 1950s and 1960s – there's suddenly room for an extended synth solo. The sound is the mellower vibe of the opening, though now it goes on extended runs. As the song does its long fade, we hear Byrne's acoustic guitar jamming with Frantz and Scales – a few friends grooving on a riff: a reminder of how the music came into being in the first place.

'Making Flippy Floppy' (Lyrics: Byrne; Music Byrne, Frantz, Harrison, Weymouth)
'Everybody, get in line', Byrne commands as a synthesizer sweeps us into the song. A flurry of Byrnian verbiage follows on this song with a title that suggests just how comic the singer sometimes found the act of sexual intercourse. His vocal sounds slightly strained, as though he's sung too many takes, trying to get the feeling just right. The music mostly hangs around two chords just a half-step apart: G7 and G#7. As was the case with the songs on *Remain In Light*, this track is more notable for its rhythmic drive than its melody. Nevertheless, with Frantz and Weymouth in the pocket, Alex Weir on a very fly rhythm guitar part, and L. Shankar playing a snaky violin, there's a catchy pulse beneath the puzzling lyrics.

Of the words on *Speaking In Tongues*, Byrne said in a radio interview that they 'are kind of hard to figure out', but they 'are meant to give a strong feeling' and 'They just try to give an impression'. We know that his compositional method at this time was to sing nonsense phrases along with instrumental jams until he had a lyric he found interesting. Individual couplets often make sense, but they don't always connect with what comes before or after, as in the conclusion of the first chorus: 'Bring me a doctor/I have a hole in my head/But they are just people/And I'm not afraid'. Obviously, it's possible to concoct a narrative out of almost any written material, but with Byrne so insistent that he's not playing Bob Dylan, it makes more sense to, as in the next track he was to sing, 'Stop making sense'.

That said, Byrne does 'give an impression' in 'Making Flippy Floppy', as in so many of his other songs, of a man torn between opposites ('Set someone free/Break someone's heart'), yet who is also given to big pronouncements ('We are born without eyesight/We are born without sin') and sudden unexpected actions ('Lock the door, we kill the beast/Kill it'.) And for those arguing that Byrne is looking beyond himself on this album, there are the lines 'Our president's crazy/Did you hear what he said?'

Of course, it may all be nothing more than what goes on in the singer's complicated mind when he is – as he tells us near the end of the song – 'Making flippy floppy/Trying to do my best'.

'Girlfriend Is Better' (Lyrics: Byrne; Music: Byrne, Frantz, Harrison, Weymouth)
This song is (sort of) in the tradition of rock-and-roll songs touting the excellence of that special someone over the merits of everyone else, with Billy 'The Kid' Emerson's 'Red Hot' probably being the premiere example: 'My gal is red hot/Your gal ain't doodly squat'. But you wouldn't know 'Girlfriend Is Better' was about a girlfriend from the opening two verses. Byrne seems to be doing his usual probing and wondering: 'Who took the money?' 'What was the place?/What was the name?' The first verse also contains one of his most memorable lines: 'It's always showtime/Here at the edge of the stage'. It's not until the chorus that we learn about the girlfriend with 'bows in her hair'. 'And nothing is better than that', Byrne states before questioning that assertion in the aside, 'Is it?' The three subsequent choruses end with Byrne declaring he has a girlfriend who is 'better than that' (whatever 'that' is) before, in very Byrnian fashion, he undercuts his avowal with similarly ambiguous statements: 'There she goes', 'Wait a minute' and, again, 'Is it?'

Appropriately, the music, while eminently danceable, has just an edge of menace or perhaps peril. The trebly rhythm guitar is matched with Bernie Worrell's deep-toned synthesizer. Other keyboard sounds – including a sci-fi laser-like effect during the chorus – give variety to the otherwise repetitive music dominated by a minor chord, which at the end of each couplet has a walk-down of A, G, F and E. The pattern stays the same for both verse and chorus.

As was the case in the first two songs, the outro is an extended instrumental: in this instance, a bubbly, almost comic synthesizer solo accompanied by electronic noises of varying truculence and intensity. As the track fades, a key line from earlier in the song may continue to ring in the ears of listeners: 'Nothing is lost/Everything's free'. It's an appropriate aesthetic statement for a band capable of reusing the same musical materials over the course of an album, but in each song, finding ways to make those materials sound different, open and free.

'Slippery People' (Lyrics: Byrne; Music: Byrne, Frantz, Harrison, Weymouth)
The album's shortest song is also one of its catchiest and funniest. Beginning with Weymouth's syncopated bass line playing against Frantz's understated drumming, keyboard and rhythm guitar soon enter to provide color, and then Byrne is off on one of his wild imaginary journeys, with lines like 'Put away that gun/This part is simple/Try to recognize what is in your mind' and 'I remember when sitting in the tub/Pulled the plug, the water was running

out'. A big chorus of voices led by Nona Hendryx and Dolette McDonald joins to accent key phrases and respond in the chorus to Byrne's statements. 'What's the matter with him?' he asks, and the chorus replies, 'He's alright'. 'I see his face' elicits the rejoinder, 'The Lord won't mind'. The chorus is sung five times, and by the end, it feels as though we've been in some strange church listening to one of its cornerstone gospel shouts. Indeed, 'Slippery People' – later covered by The Staple Singers, among others – has frequently prompted religious interpretations. The central image is a wheel turning inside a wheel, which refers specifically to a vision by Ezekiel. The Lord comes to him in a great cloud of fire, and among the revelations He visits on the prophet are the 'living creatures' (Ezekiel 1:13) (referenced in verse two) and 'a wheel in the middle of a wheel' (1:16).

There's a deep, dark hole of conjecture down which an interpreter might go, so let's simply say that the words of Ezekiel, like those of Byrne, are open to interpretation. But what's certain is that both of these figures evoke great devotion in those who follow them.

'I Get Wild/Wild Gravity' (Lyrics: Byrne; Music: Byrne, Frantz, Harrison, Weymouth)
David Fricke wrote in his *Rolling Stone* review of *Speaking In Tongues* that the music in 'I Get Wild/Wild Gravity' 'alludes to the funky voodoo reggae of Grace Jones and is heightened by arty dub intrusions and electronic handclaps'. That's certainly true as far as it goes. There's no doubt the music could be called funky voodoo reggae – Weymouth's bass line surely owes something to her time hanging out with Robbie Shakespeare in the Caribbean. Yet the blatantly sexual Grace Jones might not be the first artist who springs to mind as a corollary for Byrne. Nevertheless, as Fricke suggests, the music is less lively than on other tracks, which is appropriate for someone providing an amazingly specific description of an almost out-of-body experience, whether it's due to drugs, mental illness, or simply being cognitively different.

In the opening verse, the singer sees 'someone's face/Pleasantly out of proportion' and finds it 'hard to hold onto the ground'. In the second verse, he tells someone to 'Go ahead and pull the curtains/Check to see if I'm still here'. The third verse finds him meditating on 'Feelings without explanations' and trying unsuccessfully to describe 'The sound of a cigarette burning'.

The choruses similarly see the singer losing his grasp on reality. In the A chorus, he's bedazzled by colored lights and 'can hardly talk'. In the B Chorus, he's 'Climbing up the wall' while wondering, 'How did I get home?' Byrne's personae are often quite lost, but this one seems especially disoriented.

One of the elements that made 'Life During Wartime' so unique in the Talking Heads canon was its reference to specific locales: 'Heard about Houston/Heard about Detroit/Heard about Pittsburgh, PA'. Normally, a place for Byrne is generalized, but 'I Get Wild/Wild Gravity' tells us that he's 'Somewhere in South Carolina/And gravity don't mean a thing'. The reference to South Carolina – the birthplace of the Civil War – could suggest the conflict going on between the singer and his ability to make sense of the world. Alternately, Byrne may have included the state just because its name sounded cool when he was sifting through the mounds of random lines he generated while composing the track. It's a Talking Heads song: lyrical provenance is open to debate.

'Swamp' (Lyrics: Byrne; Music: Byrne, Frantz, Harrison, Weymouth)
Side two begins with the loping, good-time funk of 'Swamp', with Byrne initially mumbling words that are nearly impossible to decipher. (Visit any fan forum to see the wildly different interpretations.) Byrne explained in a later interview that he wrote the song 'after I'd seen a theater performance by a kind of avant-garde New York theater group called Mabou Mines. They'd done a piece called *Dead End Kids* about ... the history of nuclear power from Madame Curie to whatever, and they related it to a kind of Pandora's Box. I like that, and I like that metaphor. In order to have all this weaponry and technology, you had to make a little bit of a deal with the Devil. So that inspired the lyrics and kind of inspired the vocal treatment'.

There *are* references to nuclear apocalypse very clearly at the beginning of verse two – 'And when they split those atoms/It's hotter than the sun', and more metaphorically in the third: 'Everyone wants to explode'. The song is also rife with other unsettling imagery that might allude to nuclear holocaust. There is verse one's bag of bones in the Devil's pocket and more bones in the third, although 'Rattle them bones' could also refer to playing dice. (We also recall that Ezekiel visited a valley of bones (37:1-14), where the Lord told him he could make bones come alive.) Blood is mentioned three times, first as a 'special substance', then as something that can 'swallow you whole', and finally in the line, 'All that blood will never cover that mess'.

Electronic accents aside, the music is as close to gutbucket blues as Talking Heads ever came, at least on this album. Listen on your phone's tiny speaker, and you'll really hear the searing electric guitar line that is somewhat less prominent when the other instruments are in full throat.

Perhaps the most striking feature of 'Swamp' is Byrne's vocal register. As noted earlier, he begins by mumbling, and then he sings at the very bottom of his range as though he were pretending to be a creature from the swamp or perhaps even that Devil with a plan in the opening verse. As for the introductory mumbling, psychology professor David Sherman believes it may be Byrne reanimating his preacher persona, and a number of listeners have suggested that the singer is, appropriately, speaking in tongues.

'Moon Rocks' (Lyrics: Byrne; Music: Byrne, Frantz, Harrison, Weymouth)
An introductory percussion fill leads to Alex Weir's rhythm guitar, but the musical element that lingers longest here is Weymouth's ingenious, minimalist

bass part. She's always been a master of knowing when *not* to play, but she takes the pregnant pause to new glories here. The bass starts with the notes B, D, E, and then... wait for it... she hits her instrument's lowest E before returning to the opening figure. Towards the end, she adds a few notes to the beginning of the riff, but the pause remains. Waiting for that fourth note is hypnotic, even if you're not conscious of doing so.

The lyric was inspired by a memory from Byrne's childhood in Baltimore, where they had moon rocks in the Smithsonian, 'which was just an hour's drive away. So I imagine somebody eating one, and then this voice comes out of their stomach, and that's what the song is about'. It's a weird premise for a song, no doubt, but the lyric seems to support Byrne's claim: 'You can hear my belly rumble/There's a voice that starts to mumble/Woo! It's starting to sing' and 'I got a rock in my throat/Upside, upside down/My tummy start to talk/(What it say?)'.

There's plenty more Byrnian strangeness piled atop this already very unlikely concept. The consumption of the moon rock seems to allow the singer to believe he can levitate, and it gives him what might be termed 'special boogie powers', which make him irresistible to the ladies: 'Gonna rock it till I shock it/Gonna kick it till I drop it/ Woo! Love at first sight'. As he notes in the final verse, 'I got wild imagination, talking transubstantiation/Any version will do'.

'Pull Up The Roots' (Lyrics: Byrne; Music: Byrne, Frantz, Harrison, Weymouth)
The drumming here is much more regular, with synthesizer bass with lots of pitch bending. *This Must Be Talking Heads* host Rodney Gordon calls 'Pull Up The Roots' 'maybe the closest Talking Heads ever came to a disco song'. There's a lot of instrumental ornamentation. For the solo, initially, everyone drops out but Frantz, Weymouth and percussionist Raphael Dejesus, then Weir's unstoppable rhythm guitar returns before Byrne sings the final verse and chorus.

The title is sung 14 times, so it's clearly the key to understanding the song. *Planting* roots is generally considered to be a positive action, whether it's the literal act or the metaphorical undertaking of settling in somewhere and becoming part of a community. But for Byrne, pulling up the roots seems to be an act of eliminating a memory of something unpleasant or starting over altogether.

In the album's final track, we'll hear Byrne singing a love song far more sincere than we're used to hearing from him as he celebrates his relationship with his then-wife-to-be Adelle Lutz. Perhaps that romantic outpouring is foreshadowed here in the penultimate song. Yes, there are qualifiers like 'Someone must have been high' and 'What do I know? What do I know?' but the lyric also speaks of 'a wonderful place' where the singer can't 'wait to be'. Significantly, he tells the person he's addressing, 'I'll take you there, I'll take you there'. For the David Byrne of the previous four studio albums, that's downright sentimental.

'This Must Be The Place (Naive Melody)' (Lyrics: Byrne; Music: Byrne, Frantz, Harrison, Weymouth)
While the instrumentation here is of a piece with the rest of the album, the track – like 'The Big Country' (the closing number on *More Songs About Buildings And Food*) – is significantly different in tone. Although 'This Must Be The Place' only reached 62 on the *Billboard* Hot 100, its lovely, lilting *naïve* melody ('Naïve Melody' was originally the title) has far outlasted more popular songs on the *Billboard* chart that week in December 1983, such as Olivia Newton-John's 'Twist Of Fate' and Barry Manilow's 'Read 'Em And Weep'.

Frantz describes the composition of 'This Must Be The Place' in *Remain In Love*: 'Tina played rhythm guitar, Jerry played keyboard bass, and David played some freaky little sounds on the Prophet-5 using the modulation wheel. I played the drums because no one else knew how'.

In a 2016 episode of the YouTube series *Synth Sounds*, William Kirk goes into some depth describing those 'freaky little sounds' on what was at the time a cutting-edge synthesizer: 'one of the first polysynths with patch memory'. Kirk calls the initial lead sound a 'nuanced brass meets a steel drum type of flavor ... with maybe a little bit of a flute'. He describes the second lead that takes over the melody nearly a minute in as 'a two-oscillator saw wave sound that sounds very much like a trumpet', with 'the pitch-bend wheel very pivotal to this part of the song'.

While the unforgettable melodic hook may be primarily responsible for the song's success, it's the lyric that surprised longtime fans and won the band new devotees. Though in David Gans' *Talking Heads: The Band & Their Music*, Byrne protested that the lines were mostly 'non-sequiturs, phrases that may have a strong emotional resonance, but don't have any narrative qualities', he also admitted 'It's a real honest kind of love song. I don't think I've ever done a real love song before. Mine always had a sort of reservation or a twist. I tried to write one that wasn't corny, that didn't sound stupid or lame the way many do. I think I succeeded. I was pretty happy with that'.

The song is so familiar that it's hard to hear it with new ears, but the opening synthesizer part still sounds as fresh, innocent and optimistic as ever. When Byrne begins singing, his lyric may be composed of non-sequiturs, but they paint a consistent picture nonetheless. Like so many of Byrne's narrators, this one is confused, but he is open to seeing the good in life. Granted, he may be 'numb' and may have been 'born with a weak heart', but he still reckons he 'must be having fun'. That sense of acceptance and happiness that can only come through romantic love really kicks into gear in the chorus, where Byrne states he has 'plenty of time' and his beloved has the light in her eyes. The return of the melody halfway through leads to the second verse and chorus, which contain some of the most joyful lyrics Byrne wrote for Talking

Heads. He's been looking for a home, but he suddenly realizes he's 'already there', with a woman who has 'lifted up her wings' and shown him that 'this must be the place'.

That final long drawn-out 'Ooo' as the song moves toward the fade-out is one of pure bliss: a perfect place to end the album.

Talking Heads ... *On Track*

Stop Making Sense (Live) (1984)

Personnel
David Byrne: guitar, vocals
Chris Frantz: drums, vocals
Jerry Harrison: guitar, keyboards, vocals
Tina Weymouth: bass guitar, synth bass, guitar, vocals
Bernie Worrell: keyboards
Alex Weir: guitar, vocals
Steve Scales: percussion
Ednah Holt, Lynn Mabry: backing vocals
Producers: Talking Heads, Gary Goetzman
Recorded at Pantages Theatre, Hollywood, CA, between 13 and 16 December
1983
Label: Sire, Warner Bros.
Release date: September 1984
Running time: 39:37 (LP); 85:00 (expanded CD reissue)
Album charts: US: 41, UK: 24
Singles charts: 'Slippery People (Live)', UK: 68; 'Girlfriend Is Better (Live)', UK:
99; 'Once In A Lifetime (Live)', US: 91; 'This Must Be The Place (Naive Melody)
(Live)', UK: 100

By all accounts, the tour to promote *Speaking In Tongues* found the band and
their accompanists Bernie Worrell on keys, Alex Weir on guitar, Steve Scales
on percussion, and Ednah Holt and Lynn Mabry on backing vocals, at their
best. When director Jonathan Demme caught one of their shows, he knew he
wanted to film them. Luckily for fans of rock and roll, it all came together.

In his *Rolling Stone* review of the album, Christopher Connelly wrote
'While *The Name of This Band Is Talking Heads* was an ambitious attempt to
sum up their career-long evolution from pop minimalists to preppie
funkateers, *Stop Making Sense* assays a simpler task: to capture America's
best band ... at their peak'.

The movie is frequently cited as one of the best, if not *the* very best,
concert film ever made. And let's be honest, the film, far more than the
record, is the most memorable artifact of those four nights in December
1983 at the Pantages Theatre in Los Angeles, where a bevy of cameras
filmed the band. It's nice to have an audio version, certainly, but what's
special about *Stop Making Sense* is what director Jonathan Demme brought
to the screen. (Skip the record, Robert Christgau advised in his 1984 *Village
Voice* review: 'Buy the video'.)

Demme focused solely on the group as they appeared onstage. There are
only a few crowd shots at the very end and nothing at all capturing the band
before or after the show – no backstage shots of the group getting ready in
the dressing room before being led with a flashlight down narrow corridors
to the stage, no ruminations about the band's history or future, no critics or

74

contemporaries chiming in: just Talking Heads playing their music. Rather than what Jonathan Gould called in *The New Yorker* 'The rhythmic, fast-paced, jump-cut style of editing associated with the music videos being shown on the recently established platform MTV', we were simply given great virtual seats to a fabulous rock show, often up there among the performers.

As Matt Mitchell wrote in a 2024 *Paste* piece, 'From the bare stage to his unorthodox lighting choices (during 'Girlfriend Is Better', a crew member uses a handheld light to make shadows in the background behind the band), to the candid close-ups of each player, the filmmaker's choices were technically impressive and never too pretentious – always in service of the band and the music, never of his own selfish pursuits'.

The film cost a little over $1,000,000 to make and took in more than $5,000,000 during its initial run. It received a huge boost in 2023 when the original negative was reprocessed in high-resolution 4K format, with the film re-release earning the band nearly $7,000,000. The re-release was accompanied by group interviews with all four members, something that hadn't occurred since 1979. Each member owned 25% of the movie, so they had good reason to work together in marketing the fresh cut. Past grievances were temporarily forgiven.

In one interview, Weymouth sums up the group's working relationship on the tour: 'Sometimes it would seem very competitive, but it was good. Complacency is the worst thing to happen in a band, so we liked that we had this platter of ideas, and it was everybody trying to get them in but not clutter it up. That was important on stage, too'.

The movie includes 16 songs, three of them by *splinter* versions of the band: David Byrne's 'What A Day That Was' and 'Big Business', and Tom Tom Club's 'Genius Of Love'. The only one to make the cut for the original live album was 'What A Day That Was'. So, while this book doesn't cover Byrne's solo work, the song is – by virtue of its inclusion on this album – a *de facto* Talking Heads track and will receive extended coverage below.

As in the discussion of *The Name Of This Band Is Talking Heads*, the comments below are limited to the tracks on the original LP/Cassette/CD. Aside from the opening number, the songs on the LP do not appear in the same order as in the film, where Byrne begins playing solo with his acoustic guitar and a boombox, then is joined by one new additional band member on subsequent songs: first Weymouth, then Frantz, Harrison, and finally the other musicians. While it is a joyous concert film and album, *Stop Making Sense* represents the end of an era. Although they were clearly playing as well as any rock band in the world, this was Talking Heads' final tour. In the years to come, Frantz, Weymouth and Harrison wanted to take the band's music to live audiences, but Byrne could not be persuaded.

'Psycho Killer' (Byrne, Frantz, Weymouth)
Byrne begins the album and the film by saying, 'Hi, I've got a tape I want to play'. Then he presses the Play button on a boombox he's set down on the

stage, and we hear a rudimentary drum track (which is annoyingly high in the audio mix). All alone on an empty stage, Byrne begins playing his acoustic guitar and singing the album or film's only number from *Talking Heads: 77*. It's something of a revelation. There's an acoustic version on the expanded CD release of their first album, but it's played by the full band, with the addition of cellist Arthur Russell. Byrne's solo *Stop Making Sense* rendition highlights the strange purity of his unusual voice.

'Swamp' (Lyrics: Byrne; Music: Byrne, Frantz, Harrison, Weymouth)
In the film, the next song is 'Heaven', with Byrne joined by Weymouth on bass. But on the 1984 album pressing, we jump all the way to the ninth song, by which time the full expanded band has been on stage for three songs. On-screen, Byrne marches in place in front of a red backdrop, which, with his slicked-back 1930s-era hair, feels vaguely fascistic. Between marching, he limps along the stage like a cripple, and his affected deeper-than-normal voice gives the entire song the weird vibe it demands. It's a drums-and-keyboard-driven track, with Weymouth playing the synthesizer bass. The song is well-executed, though, in its audio version, it's not materially different from the track released on *Speaking In Tongues* the year before.

'Slippery People' (Lyrics: Byrne; Music: Byrne, Frantz, Harrison, Weymouth)
This is the fifth song in the film and the first one with musicians not in the core band: Steve Scales on percussion and Ednah Holt and Lynn Mabry on backing vocals. Byrne actually smiles during many parts of the song, and Holt and Mabry – dressed in what look like chic grey workout clothes – bring a ton of energy, visually and vocally. (This is the song where they play air guitar, mimicking Byrne as he rocks back and forth.) Once Bernie Worrell takes the stage, he mostly crowds Harrison out of the keyboard spotlight. But in 'Slippery People', Harrison is given a brief, magical solo. Something's certainly lost without the visual, but this is a solid, energetic version of the original, with Scales' percussion being a highlight.

'Burning Down The House' (Lyrics: Byrne; Music: Byrne, Frantz, Harrison, Weymouth)
Guitarist Alex Weir had joined the band onstage on the previous song 'Cities', but this, the film's seventh song, is the first to feature Bernie Worrell on keyboards. Released just six months earlier and still wildly popular, Talking Heads' highest-charting single received a rapturous welcome at the Pantages Theatre. Weymouth is back on the synthesizer bass, and Byrne plays acoustic guitar, accompanied by an amped-up and dancing Alex Weir on electric. (At one point, they stand next to each other, running in place with what looks like endless vitality.) It's a rocking version of the song, with band members clearly drawing from each other's excitement. Does it *sound* as good as it

looks on screen? Well, no. But like 'Slippery People', 'Burning Down The House' holds its own against the studio original.

'Girlfriend Is Better' (Lyrics: Byrne; Music: Byrne, Frantz, Harrison, Weymouth)
The fourth song in a row from *Speaking In Tongues* and the final track from that album to make the original *Stop Making Sense* LP, 'Girlfriend Is Better' provided the project's title, with the phrase sung a total of five times toward the end of the song. The line 'It's always showtime here at the edge of the stage' is a perfect statement of the tour and the film's aesthetic, as we see Byrne wander onstage in his Noh-inspired Big Suit, which became the iconic image from *Stop Making Sense*. 'Girlfriend Is Better' is the third-to-last song in the film, and it comes right after Weymouth and Frantz have had their star turn playing Tom Tom Club's hit 'Genius Of Love', so it makes sense that Byrne would want to upstage them. For the first part of the song, only he is in the spotlight, with the rest of the ensemble toiling away in semi-darkness. Worrell's keyboard solos are fun to hear, but they pale in comparison to the crazy dancing Byrne is doing onstage and onscreen in his oversized clothing.

'Once In A Lifetime' (Lyrics: Byrne; Music: Byrne, Frantz, Harrison, Weymouth, Eno)
The first song on side 2 is the original LP's only song from *Remain In Light*. The 12th song in the film, 'Once In A Lifetime' is sequenced after the band is warmed up and rocking, and it presents as a fuller version than the *Remain In Light* songs on *The Name Of This Band Is Talking Heads*. Keyboards and bass provide a funky bottom end, and Holt and Mabry's vocals are superb. It's an excellent take, arguably as strong as – or stronger than – the original. On stage, Byrne wears nerdy horn-rim glasses as he jerks spastically to the music, occasionally fake-hitting himself in the head. In the background, you can see Frantz singing along *sans* microphone, simply enjoying being part of a great band.

'What A Day That Was' (Byrne)
This song from *The Catherine Wheel* begins with Weymouth's thumping bass and Harrison and Worrell's funky keyboard riffs. Quickly, Byrne begins singing, and then it's time to hold on to your hats because, like many of Byrne's best lyrics, this one is complex and open to a wide variety of interpretations.

The opening lines – 'I'm dressed up so nice/And I'm doing my best/Yes, I'm starting over/Starting over in another place' – sound quaintly autobiographical. But in the next verse, we are with a 'Big Chief with a golden crown' and 'rings on his fingers'. The chief is 'making shapes with his hands', and we are told that we dare not sit back, sit down, or speak up. Have we been transported to some exotic tribe, or been sent deep into history, or is the big chief God himself? The chorus, supported by Holt and Mabry's huge backing vocals, is intriguing but inconclusive: 'And on the first day we had everything we could stand/Who could have asked for more?/And on the second day there was nothing else left to do/Oooh what a day that was'. (In the two subsequent verses, Byrne changes the penultimate line to the less optimistic 'There was nothing else left at all'.) One possible reading is that the narrator has been witnessing or participating in the creation of the Universe. But in his telling, what took God six days is compressed into just one, with the day of rest as the song's focus.

In the following verse, we are confronted with '50,000 beggars roaming in the streets'. In the verse after that, which seems to support the idea of the Big Chief as God or *a* god, a lightning bolt comes down and starts an electrical storm. In the final verse before the chorus, we learn that the singer has been 'dreaming of a city/It was my own invention', which again suggests that he is a part of, or at one with, the great creator.

The bridge provides us with the encouraging news that 'There's a million ways to make things work out'. But after a brief keyboard solo, the final three verses shake things up even further. First, we hear 'They're rounding them up from all over town': possibly alluding to the homeless beggars. Then unnamed individuals are 'moving forward and backwards', and ultimately 'You feel like you're in a whirlpool', but you may also be interested in 'talking to someone who knows the difference between right and wrong'. The outro, with words based on the rhyming of 'boom, boom, boom' and 'great big room', doesn't explain much unless that great big room is Heaven.

Whatever the lyric means, Byrne, as we know, frequently claimed that the sound of words was just as important as their sense. The music itself is unstoppable, with Alex Weir playing a mean slide and, along with Byrne, rhythm guitar.

In the film, everyone is up-lit so that shadows and darkness are as much a part of the song as glimpses of the musicians' faces. Towards the end, we see their shadows jiving in time on the screen in the background – a well-oiled dance machine that would have made Talking Heads' early heroes KC and the Sunshine Band proud.

'Life During Wartime' (Byrne, Frantz, Harrison, Weymouth)
In the film, 'Life During Wartime' comes just after 'Burning Down The House', and the audience is still jacked up and cheering. The only song from *Fear Of Music* on the original LP, the *Stop Making Sense* rendition is even more full of energy than its studio predecessor. However, a significant part of that energy is only conveyed on screen, where we see the entire front line (Holt, Mabry, Byrne, Weymouth and Weir) jogging in time to the music. Shed off his normal-sized suit jacket before donning the big one, Byrne makes the most of his slim frame to engage in a variety of dance maneuvers and acrobatics, including falling on his back like an upended turtle. In the longer version in

the film and on 1984 CDs and cassettes, rather than ending after the singing, the song continues with some zippy synthesizer runs while Byrne jogs and runs around the entire stage. It's a cardio workout for sure, whether you can see or only hear the song.

'Take Me To The River' (Green, Hodges)
This penultimate song in the 16-song movie (a guitar-drenched 'Crosseyed And Painless' is the finale) is a natural album closer. Like 'Psycho Killer', it's an early song beloved by true fans and casual listeners alike. 'Psycho Killer' and 'Take Me To The River' are the only two songs to appear on the original releases of both live albums. However, where the earlier live version of 'Psycho Killer' was performed by the four-piece band, the previous live 'Take Me To The River' also received the expanded-ensemble treatment. The versions are not dissimilar, both drawing the ending out significantly. But the song is played faster in *Stop Making Sense*, and it's nice to hear the brief solos by Weir on guitar and Harrison on keyboards. Of course, if we're watching the film, we get to see the band revel in the triumph of nearly reaching the conclusion of a wildly successful concert, which is definitely a sight not to miss.

Talking Heads ... On Track

Little Creatures (1985)

Personnel:
David Byrne: guitar, vocals
Chris Frantz: drums
Jerry Harrison: keyboards, guitar, backing vocals
Tina Weymouth: bass, backing vocals
Andrew Cader: washboard ('Road To Nowhere')
Gordon Grody, Lani Groves, Kurt Yahjian: backing vocals
Ellen Bernfeld: backing vocals ('Perfect World', 'Walk It Down')
Erin Dickens: backing vocals ('Television Man', 'Road To Nowhere')
Diva Gray: backing vocals ('Road To Nowhere')
Jimmy Macdonell: accordion ('Road To Nowhere')
Lenny Pickett: saxophone
Steve Scales: percussion
Naná Vasconcelos: percussion ('Perfect World')
Eric Weissberg: pedal steel ('Creatures Of Love', 'Walk It Down')
Producer: Talking Heads
Release date: 10 June 1985
Recorded: October 1984, March 1985
Studio: Sigma Sound, New York City
Label: Sire
Running time: 38:38
Album charts: US 20; UK 10
Singles charts: 'The Lady Don't Mind', UK: 81; 'Road To Nowhere', UK: 6; 'And She Was', US: 54, UK 17

In a 2021 interview with Rodney Gordon, Jerry Harrison recalled the genesis of *Little Creatures*:

> *Little Creatures* were the outtakes of the songs that David was writing for *True Stories*, and yet I do think it's a superior album by actually quite a long shot. When we mixed *Little Creatures*, at the same time, we rehearsed all the basic tracks for all the songs for *True Stories* and recorded them in between our mixes ... And David had very deliberately, because of the nature of what he wanted to do with *True Stories*, had written his version of sort of Americana, I would call it. So the songs are not as poly-rhythmic, they're not as contrapuntal, they don't require so many people to play. There was a sense of wanting to just be straightforward but also maybe a little more pop.

In *The Band And Their Music*, Weymouth notes that the group had not played together for more than a year before they began rehearsing again. After *Stop Making Sense* was made, 'we didn't know where to go ... For one thing, David got really interested in becoming a movie star and a director, scriptwriter and everything to do with movies. Jerry's been working on his second album, and

80

I've been a housewife and a mother'. On *Little Creatures*, they are 'just four people singing some easy, simple songs with no pretensions of being avant-garde, African or any of that'. Frantz echoed his wife's slightly dismissive tone when discussing the record. The songs 'sound very sweet'. They 'have nice, pretty melodies and harmonies'. The rhythm section, in short, is – other than on a couple of tracks – no longer involved in the composition of the music.

Byrne wrote the songs on acoustic guitar and drum machine. As he says in *How Music Works*, 'I decided to write them ahead of the recording sessions, in what now seemed to us the old-fashioned way: playing a guitar and singing along'.

Overall, despite songs like 'Little Creatures', in which children come to resemble little monsters, and 'Stay Up All Night', where the singer insists that a baby not go to sleep so that the adults can play with him, the album was generally seen as a step toward maturity. Originally titled *In Defense Of Television*, *Little Creatures* – like previous Talking Heads albums – was concerned with the effect media had on people's perceptions of the world around them. In fact, two of the band's most memorable videos were taken from this album. 'And She Was' is a visual feast, and 'Stay Up Late', rather than telling a story that might be interpreted as child abuse, shows the band members in white jumpsuits flying around a cavernous space while attached to cables.

Produced by the band with engineer Eric Thorngreen, *Little Creatures* has a big sound even though the instrumentation is relatively minimal compared to *Speaking In Tongues* and *Stop Making Sense*. There are horns and boogaloo-inflected percussion, synthesizers and lots of soaring backing vocals. In short, while critics echoed Harrison's comment about this set of songs being Byrne's take on Americana, *Little Creatures* is hardly an album by The Jayhawks or Roseanne Cash.

Outsider artist Reverend Howard Finster of Summerville, Georgia, was commissioned to paint the album cover. He described his assignment as follows: 'The one that sings for them, he sent me a picture o' him and the other ones in the group, and he wanted to draw him holdin' up the world'. Indeed, that's exactly what Finster did. Although the person holding the globe on his shoulders doesn't look much like Byrne, we know it's him because Finster has helpfully penned the name David on the underpants the singer is wearing (his only clothing besides a pair of shoes.) Elsewhere on the cover, the other members – also labeled with their names – sit among a dizzying world of smiling and frowning clouds, mountains, churches, towers, leopards and flying saucers.

The back cover shows the band standing at attention, hands at their sides, dressed in wildly-colored clothes. Frantz wears a pink suit coat with crushed green velvet pants. Harrison's trousers are decorated with yellow, pink and blue seashells. Byrne's jacket is practically exploding with flowers, while Weymouth is dressed in several skirts and blue trousers with a tartan tam-o'-shanter atop her head.

While some critics rightly heard *Little Creatures* as a retrenchment from the experimentation of *Remain In Light* and the high energy of *Speaking In Tongues* and *Stop Making Sense*, like all Talking Heads albums, it was generally well-received by the scribbling class. Rob Tannenbaum wrote in his *Rolling Stone* review: '*Little Creatures* is the sound of David Byrne falling in love with normalcy. Though this is a modest, enchanting album, those who equate creativity with complexity will undoubtedly dismiss it as old wave. But with the rest of the pop world still catching up to the brilliant *Remain In Light*, what could be more subversive than a clean and happy record?'

Robert Christgau awarded the album an A grade:

What the relatively straight and spare approach signifies is that their expansive '80s humanism doesn't necessarily require pluralistic backup or poly-rhythmic underpinnings. It affirms that compassionate grownups can rock and roll. The music is rich in hidden treasures the way their punk-era stuff never was, and though the lyrics aren't always crystalline, their mysteries seem more like poetry than obscurantism this time out.

Their second platinum album (after *Speaking In Tongues), Little Creatures* ultimately became the band's most successful album, selling more than 2,000,000 copies in the United States.

'And She Was' (Byrne)

The first song begins with a shouted 'Hey!' and it's off from there into a track that is practically irresistible. Musically, the catchy chorus echoes the heart and soul of 'Not Fade Away', 'Gloria', 'Wild Thing' and a thousand other garage-band standards. The bridge changes things slightly and then it's back to basics, the song churning on, relentlessly upbeat.

In several interviews, Byrne said the lyric was inspired by a girl he knew who took LSD near a factory, and that does mesh with the story in the first verse. 'A new kind of religion being born out of heaps of rusted cars and fast-food joints', he says in the liner notes to *Once In A Lifetime*. 'And this girl was flying above it all, but in it too'. It's equally plausible that 'she' is actually physically rising from the earth in a moment of saint-like ecstasy. In Carlos Eire's *They Flew: A History Of The Impossible*, we learn that levitation is frequently the result of being enraptured by God, and the title character *does* appear to be in the midst of a truly spiritual experience. (Byrne obviously was intrigued by the topic – think of the 'Flying saucers, levitation/Yo! I could do that' in *Speaking In Tongues*' 'Moon Rocks'.) The chorus, especially, emphasizes the woman's convergence with the planet's orbital rhythms, with the verses suggesting her ability to transcend them.

The music is uplifting, and the lines about joining with the universe make the song feel jubilant. That is, until the very end, when we learn that the woman's floating off into the universe means she is 'Joining the world of missing persons'. Even as the outro continues with its buoyant title repetition, we can't help but feel that something worrying has occurred.

While the song plateaued at 54 in the United States, it did much better in the UK (17), and it has had a long afterlife partly due to the brilliant video created by Jim Blashfield, which imaginatively and faithfully recreated the woman's flight across the sky using what look like photocopied images – her painted toenails floating above houses, trees, clouds, chimneys, streetlights, shuttlecocks and newspaper kites. It's a fantastical journey, and while I've tried to avoid using music videos to explain the audio versions of the band's songs, this one functions in a virtuous circle with the track, each amplifying and augmenting the other.

'Give Me Back My Name' (Lyrics: Byrne; Music: Byrne, Frantz, Harrison, Weymouth)
Two repeating minor chords a half step apart give this opening a much different feeling than the opening song. Still, it's not exactly the single-chord focus of *Remain In Light*. The playing is too straightforward. These are real guitars, not wigged-out synthesizers or effects-laden axes *à la* Adrian Belew. Weymouth sings along with Byrne, though by her own admission, she has 'a very, very small voice'.

The track is relatively short, with many repeated lines, so it's difficult to know just who the speaker is. Yes, he wants his name back, but who took it and why? The key lines seem to be the following:

Let X make a statement
Let breath pass through those cracked lips
That man was my hero
And now that word has been taken from us

Podcaster Rodney Gordon suggests that X might be Malcolm X (the song was recorded around the 20th anniversary of his death). However, the song seems to be primarily about language's inability to accurately communicate feelings and information.

The singer tells us, 'There's a word for it', but he immediately undercuts that statement with 'And words don't mean a thing'. We learn that 'Names make all the difference in the world', but 'Some things can never be spoken' or 'pronounced'. Indeed, the word the singer is looking for 'does not exist in any language'.

It's a deconstructionist, linguistic house of mirrors and about as far away from 'And She Was' as you can get.

Whatever the correct interpretation, 'Give Me Back My Name' changes the album's immediate tone from one of elation to something much more pensive. Listeners encountering the album for the first time must have wondered what in the world would come next.

'Creatures Of Love' (Byrne)

On an interview disc Sire created to promote the album, Weymouth recounted Byrne's description of 'Creatures Of Love': 'He was very excited. He says, 'It's a country song, and it's about when a man and a woman lie in bed and make love. When they lift the sheets off, suddenly the bed is covered with little creatures ... not babies, but ... fully formed, grown-up little creatures about six inches high ... running all over the bed'. So we said, 'Oh right, David, okay'. But then it turned out we really liked the song'.

That horror movie version of the song still echoes in the first-verse words: 'And when they lay together/Little creatures all come out'. Later, Byrne sings, 'From a moment of passion/ Now they cover the bed'. Far from seeming like a mature statement about human sexuality and reproduction from a man about to enter his 30s, 'Creatures Of Love' feels more like what Ian Gittins hilariously described in *Once In A Lifetime* as someone teaching 'sex education to a class of particularly arrested-development six-year-olds'.

At the end of the song, we get another hint of the singer's disturbing attitude toward childbirth in the line 'From the sleep of reason, a life is born', which clearly echoes the title of Goya's famous etching, 'The Sleep Of Reason Produces Monsters'. Goya's engraving shows a parliament of raging owls clustering around a dreaming man. Like the little creatures Byrne described to Weymouth, these creatures seem far from compassionate. Perhaps the closest comparison is the nightmarish, forever caterwauling organism spawned in David Lynch's 1977 film *Eraserhead*.

There's also a weird gesture on Byrne's part towards a kind of nerd-feminism. The first line tells us that 'A woman made a man', not the other way around as the book of Genesis would have us believe. And 'A man, he made a house' – if he's not a carpenter, perhaps he's a househusband? Later, we hear that 'A man can drive a car/And a woman can be a boss'. 'Well, yeah, duh', might be the response before the total bewilderment likely to follow from the next two lines: 'I'm a monkey and a flower/I'm everything at once'. Huh?

If the words are often strange, there's also a spirit of goodwill running through the song, which is accentuated by its lovely melody. Unwilling though he might have been to immerse himself in the domestic affairs of others, Byrne was nevertheless exposed to the domesticity of Weymouth and Frantz and their by-all-accounts extremely cute son Robin. At one point, Byrne almost pleads to find the mysterious way into family life:

So Doctor, Doctor
Tell me what I am
Am I one of those human beings?
Well, I can laugh, or I can learn to think
So help me now to find out what to feel
Help me now!

Again, the more benign aspects of the creatures of love are emphasized by the music, which has a good-time, mellow country feel. It all begins with the pedal steel guitar of bluegrass legend Eric Weissberg, who is of 'Dueling Banjos' fame in *Deliverance*. Country-inflected electric guitars and a simple drum rhythm carry the song along, through, over, under and past the sometimes uncomfortable lyric. A casual listener might not even register the presence of the tiny freaks. As Byrne noted in a 1985 *Spin* magazine article, 'The beauty of it was writing a ballad, instead of some spooky little monster stomp. That was the challenge'.

'The Lady Don't Mind' (Lyrics: Byrne; Music: Byrne, Frantz, Harrison, Weymouth)

'The Lady Don't Mind' begins slowly, with a guitar and synth piano call-and-response, before it heats up. Written during the *Speaking In Tongues* sessions, this is the second of the two songs on *Little Creatures* that credit all four members as writers. 'The Lady Don't Mind' has what David Bowman calls 'an infectious Ricky Ricardo rhythm and horn chart', but it is Steve Scales' percussion that really keeps things moving.

The lady of the title seems to be a cousin of the protagonist of 'And She Was'. Like the earlier character, she appears able to overcome the forces of gravity. The opening line tells us, 'Last time she jumped out the window/Well, she only turned and smiled'. Evidently, this act comes without any ill effects, for soon she is on a 'Little boat that floats on a river/It's drifting through a haze/She floats by whenever she wants to/Well, there she goes again'.

While it might be a stretch – and what interpretation of a David Byrne lyric is *not* a stretch? – the fact that the lady is in a boat and later looks in a mirror where 'She lets her feelings show' suggests the possibility that she is at least a distant relative of Tennyson's 'The Lady of Shalott', who spends her time in a castle by the river with a spinning wheel, where 'In her web she still delights/To weave the mirror's magic sights'. Of course, the Lady of Shallot falls to pieces when she finally sees her beloved Lancelot in the mirror, while the lady in this song 'don't mind' really anything at all.

As the song winds down and Byrne repeats 'Uh-oh' again and again, we can't help but recall 'Uh-Oh, Love Has Come To Town' from the first album, recorded nearly eight long years earlier. The band members are the same, but this is a very different group now – one that seems to have eschewed hard-edged experimentation in favor of the friendly confines of popular music.

'Perfect World' (Lyrics: Byrne, Frantz; Music: Byrne)

'Perfect World' grooves into being on a bluesy soul riff. Then there's quite a bit of lyric waffling: 'Well, I don't what it is/But I don't know where it is', and so on. After all the specific images we've been getting to this point, the pure abstraction of the first two verses here is somewhat off-putting, making it hard to zero in on just why the epitome of dissatisfaction has suddenly found himself in a perfect world.

In a 1985 interview in *Spin* magazine, Byrne recalled that he was 'looking through some old lyrics, and I found two couplets that Chris had written years ago: 'This is a perfect world' or 'You're a perfect girl' or something like that, and 'I'm riding on an incline/I'm staring at your face'. I changed a few of the words. It had a bit of a bizarre quality that I really liked. So I paired them with some other words that I'd written, and that became 'Perfect World''. The result is indeed a bit of a bizarre love song, though it certainly reads as a more sincere attempt to connect with a beloved than many of his efforts. Speculation is that the object of his affection is his future wife, photographer Adelle Lutz.

And those final lines sung in falsetto – 'I'm staring in your face/You'll photograph mi-i-i-ne' do have a ring of real emotion. Of course, in Byrne's world, there is no such thing as a perfect world, but in this song, he seems at least within spitting distance of it.

The soul vibe continues right to the end, with Brazilian percussionist Nana Vasconcelos adding to the fun with his water drum, which Frantz describes in *Remain In Love* as 'a handmade round ceramic pot with a hole on top that Nana would fill with a certain amount of water to create a unique wobbly, resonant sound'.

'Stay Up Late' (Byrne)

There are two main ways to understand the opening song on side two. The first and most generous envisions the speaker as a child with a new sibling or perhaps a quirky but fun-loving uncle. This person wants to make the baby 'stay up all night' out of a sense of joy and wonder. He can't get over how delightful this new (little) creature is with his 'little pee pee' and 'little toes', and he wants to play with him forever. Of course, as any parent or babysitter knows, keeping an infant up all night is a truly bad idea, and in this interpretation of the song, a responsible adult will, at some point, come along to quell the singer's enthusiasm and get the baby to bed on time.

Another darker take on the lyric is that the singer is actually responsible for the child's well-being, but most listeners of this perpetually popular song have taken the first interpretation. Parents may recall the joy of playing with their infant children and think of staying 'up all night' as a comic exaggeration. The fun Byrne seems to be having with the song suggests it's right not to take it too seriously. However, as with so many Talking Heads tracks, 'Stay Up Late' has a more negative side that cannot be ignored.

Aside from the unusual conceit of the lyric, what makes this song so catchy is the sing-along melody and sheer exuberance of everyone involved. The song consists of just four chords, but they are arranged and rearranged so we never have the feeling of being mired in a single self-contained structure *à la Remain In Light*. Harrison's piano playing and Frantz's drumming are absolutely in sync, turning 'Stay Up Late' into one of the most memorable songs in the band's catalog.

'Walk It Down' (Byrne)

This track begins with a weird synthesizer sound, which David Bowman aptly describes in *This Must Be The Place* as something like 'a monstrous *Star Wars* reptile rhythmically jiggling the flaps around its neck in time to the music'. As the drums and bass pound relentlessly forward, Byrne sings to himself, beginning with an 'I' and finishing the line with his voice through an EQ filter: 'am just a number'. Then comes 'And I/Hang on to what I got'. For a Talking Heads verse, this one is pretty bland. It feels like something you have to endure in order to reach the chorus. The pre-chorus offers some hope of a melody, but the surprise comes when this near-dirge hits the chorus and suddenly there's a real musical hook: 'I said walk it down/Talk it down/Oh, oh, oh/ Sympathy, luxury/Somebody will take you there'. It's a joyful noise, hinting at the full-throated gospel on the album's final track.

The lyric in the synth string-washed bridge is an odd amalgam of clichés – 'I bet my life/What you see is what you get' – though the singer seems to be trying to reconcile the candor of the verse ('Lies, lies and propaganda') with the presumably ironic, yuppified aspiration of the chorus.

All in all, 'Walk It Down' is an odd song. Eric Weissberg's pedal steel playing is just audible in the mix (something of a missed opportunity), though things do pick up musically with Harrison's organ playing just prior to the final choruses.

'Television Man' (Byrne)

'Television Man' makes for a nice pairing with 'Found A Job' from *More Songs About Buildings And Food*. That song told the story of Bob and Judy, an unhappy couple who saved their relationship by 'Making up their own shows' for television, with Bob frequently 'on the street ... scouting up locations' while Judy was 'in the bedroom, inventing situations'. The worldview of the 'Television Man' narrator is similarly formed by what was once called the idiot box: 'Television made me what I am'. Granted, he doesn't want to disclose just how close he is to his TV – 'We are just good friends' – but he has no qualms about announcing 'I'm a television man'. Indeed, the bridge moves the discussion to an almost heavenly plane:

> Take a walk in the beautiful garden
> Everyone would like to say hello
> It doesn't matter what you say
> Come and take us away

However, unlike Bob and Judy, the man hasn't quite found a way to make television a force for good in his life. The stop/start rhythm keeps the singer and the listener on edge. The world keeps crashing into his living room, but he can't turn away: 'I'm watching everything'.

The bridge is followed by Steve Scales taking a wild romp on percussion, with Byrne then leading the backing singers in a classic call-and-response. A sneaky guitar part joins a bell-like synthesizer, with Frantz's drums loud and accounted for and Weymouth's bass pops keeping things funky. Then, a gnarly, distorted lead guitar plays the melody. There hasn't been such an extended and complex instrumental passage in a Talking Heads song since *Remain In Light*, and it's no wonder this is the longest track on the album.

As Byrne takes us to the end, the *Saturday Night Live* bandleader and Tower Of Power sax player Lenny Pickett joins the full ensemble, resulting in a buildup that resolves into a final major chord. Clearly, the song is a critique of watching too much television; it makes folks like the song's protagonist passive and confused. But in classic Talking Heads fashion, the triumphant tone of the chorus and finale undercuts some of that censure.

'Road To Nowhere' (Byrne)

The album's final and probably strongest track begins with a choir singing *a cappella*. The lyric has a timeless quality as if it were a gospel song or perhaps a nearly forgotten tune from what Greil Marcus once called the old, weird America.

While laced with uncertainty, the opening verse offers a hopeful vibe overall, ending with the notion that, given some time and space, those on the road can figure out what they should be doing. That sense of unease (the destination is 'very far away') coupled with muted optimism ('I'm feeling okay this morning') continues throughout the song, but the music itself is jubilant, practically insisting that listeners join in and sing. As with all the tracks on *Little Creatures*, Frantz's drumming is at the forefront, and Weymouth's bass part – not often featured on the album but now as simple and urgent as an anxious heartbeat – pairs up nicely with the second-line snare.

Accordion is a particularly apt touch. Played by Jimmy Macdonnell – whose zydeco band Loup Garou had been gigging around New York – the accordion anchors the song in South Louisiana, with Harrison's organ-playing offering a solid counter-punch. Lenny Pickett's saxophone periodically fills out the sound, and Andrew Cader – a one-time floor broker on the New York Stock Exchange – plays a vigorous washboard, with spoons no less.

In the 1985 *Spin* cover story on the band, Byrne called 'Road To Nowhere' 'a kind of gospel, Cajun march. It's a happy, upbeat song; all these people singing about being on the road to oblivion'. And in the liner notes for *Once In A Lifetime: The Best Of Talking Heads*, he says he 'wanted to write a song that presented a resigned, even joyful look at doom ... The front bit – the white gospel choir – is kind of tacked on because I didn't think the rest of the song was enough. I mean, it was only two chords. So out of embarrassment or shame, I wrote an intro section that had a couple more in it'.

The result was not only what became one of the band's most recognized numbers but also a genuine contribution to the American songbook. 'Road

To Nowhere' may contain a small helping of the usual Byrnian hesitations and contradictions, but its overarching spirit can be found in the repeated phrase 'It's all right, Baby, it's all right'.

Talking Heads ... On Track

True Stories (1986)

Personnel:
David Byrne: guitar, vocals
Chris Frantz: drums
Jerry Harrison: keyboards, guitar, backing vocals
Tina Weymouth: bass, backing vocals
Bert Cross Choir: vocals ('Puzzlin' Evidence')
St. Thomas Aquinas Elementary School Choir: vocals ('Hey Now')
Tommy Camfield: fiddle ('People Like Us')
Paulinho da Costa: percussion ('Papa Legba', 'Radio Head', 'People Like Us')
Steve Jordan: accordion ('Radio Head')
Tommy Morrell: pedal steel ('People Like Us', 'City Of Dreams')
Producer: Talking Heads
Recorded between February and June 1986
Studios: Sigma Sound, New York City; O'Henry Sound, Toluca Lake, California;
Studio Southwest, Sunnyvale, Texas; The Arcadia Theater, Dallas, Texas
Release date: 15 September 1986
Running time: 40:33
Label: Sire
Album charts: US: 17, UK: 7
Singles charts: 'Wild Wild Life', US: 25, UK 43; 'Radio Head', UK: 52

The film *True Stories* is kind of funny, kind of charming and kind of dumb.
David Byrne, as the narrator, plays a version of himself: deadpan and *naïve*,
but caustically so, wandering around the imaginary town of Virgil, Texas, in a
cowboy hat as Virgil prepares to commemorate the state's sesquicentennial
with a 'Celebration of specialness'.

The movie's characters are wildly over the top. Spalding Gray plays an
executive of computer chip manufacturer Vericorp, who, for no evident
reason, only talks to his wife through their children. Tito Larriva of the Plugz
and Cruzados is a Romeo, a sometime worker at the factory and sometimes a
musician. Alix Elais plays a woman on the Vericorp integrated circuit
assembly line who can only tolerate the world when it is 'cute' and 'sweet'.
Then there's the hilarious Jo Harvey Allen, who cannot open her mouth
without telling a lie. Swoosie Kurtz plays a woman so rich and lazy that she
never has to get out of bed, thanks partly to the aid rendered by 'Pops'
Staples, who also dabbles in Haitian voodoo. John Goodman as Louis Fyne –
a man who has no luck with women but is dead-set on matrimony – steals
every scene he's in.

Byrne and his co-writer, character actor Stephen Tobolowsky (Ned, the
insurance salesman in *Groundhog Day*), along with Pulitzer Prize-winning
dramatist Beth Henley (Tobolowsky's girlfriend at the time), have a ball with
the script (the asparagus stalks in place of flowers at the Vericorp exec's
dinner table are pretty wonderful) while managing to smuggle-in some ersatz

90

philosophy: 'Shopping is a feeling', 'Economics has become a spiritual theory' and 'Often our true nature is not what we hope it is'. In short, *True Stories* is the sort of movie anyone but a Talking Heads or John Goodman fan would probably be happy to watch only once.

The album is quite different. The band's most diverse album, by a long shot, takes superb songs that were played mostly for laughs in the movie and gives them the full treatment. The result is Talking Head's most underappreciated album.

Recorded simultaneously with *Little Creatures*, *True Stories* inevitably shares qualities with it. Both records were produced by Talking Heads with Eric Thorngren engineering and mixing. Both albums have a very Byrnian take on America, with country and gospel touches that include pedal steel on several tracks and a full church choir on another. As Frantz said of the *Little Creatures* numbers, the songs have 'a beginning, a middle, and an end'. *True Stories* also shares with *Little Creatures* what feel like moments of real emotion, unencumbered by the singer's cynicism.

The album cover, designed by Michael Hodgson and Jeffrey Kent Ayeroff using a logo by Bridget DeSoccio, makes use of just three colors: black, white and red. In the top half, 'Talking' is in black font on a white background, with 'Heads' in a white font on a red background. The back cover has 'True' in white on red, with 'Stories' in black on white. (On the original vinyl LP, the side-one label had only the *True Stories* logo, while side two contained the track information for both sides, which were called 'Other Side' and 'This Side'.) It vies with Talking Heads: 77 for the simplest design of any Talking Heads album and is one of their most immediately recognizable.

Though *Remain In Light* continued to be the work of genius by which all their other records were judged, not everyone was a true believer in the landmark 1980 album. In his *Rolling Stone* review of *True Stories*, Mark Coleman wrote, 'Talking Heads continue to delve into their American musical roots, and for my money, it's a more sensible and successful mission than their pith-helmeted foray into Africa on *Remain In Light*'. But Coleman's opinion about the relative merits of *True Stories* compared to the already classic earlier albums was in the minority. Giving the album a B, Robert Christgau admitted that these were 'real songs, not detached avant-garde atmospherics'. But he felt that 'Honest though David Byrne's sympathy may (I said may) be, (the songs) leach their vitality from traditions that demand more heart than he ordinarily coughs up'.

Considering how often critics dismissed it, *True Stories* sold surprisingly well. Some of those sales might have been because six weeks after the album's release, Byrne appeared on the cover of *Time* magazine as 'Rock's Renaissance Man'. He was described as a singer, composer, lyricist, guitarist, film director, writer, actor, video artist, designer and photographer. Frantz's response to the *Time* piece – as recollected in *Remain In Love* – was not surprising. After noting that Byrne had 'hired his own publicist separate from the band', Frantz remarked, *'Really? Time* magazine put him on the cover and called him rock's renaissance man. There was some truth to it, but you know he did not get to this point alone'. Tensions were clearly building. This was to be their penultimate album. But whatever continuing resentment the others might have felt toward their frontman, *True Stories* came across as an expression of pure musical delight.

'Love For Sale' (Byrne)

Cole Porter's slow, wistful song of the same name is a far cry from the robust number that opens *True Stories*. Porter's song – which originally appeared in the 1930 musical *The New Yorkers* – was sung by a sex worker looking for business. It was a sad but romanticized version of prostitution, including the lines 'Let the poets pipe of love in their childish way/I know every type of love/Better far than they'. Ella Fitzgerald's version is a downright heartbreaker.

In contrast, 'Love For Sale' by Talking Heads is primarily about commerce, with the trappings of love being simply a way to sell products. The opening line establishes the world in which the rest of the song occurs: 'I was born in a house with the television always on'. The speaker grew up too fast and forgot his name, and this amnesia, along with excess time on his hands, appears to make him susceptible to the corporate sales pitches he's constantly barraged with. Soon, actual ad slogans become part of the Lyrics: 'Leave the driving to us' (Greyhound) and 'It's the real thing' (Coca-Cola). Then things get weird, with the singer 'rolling in the blender' with his beloved, who he plans to love 'like a color TV'.

The second verse continues the surreal twist on selling and love, with the singer telling the object of his affections, 'You can put your lipstick all over my designer jeans'. If she turns his dial, he tells her, 'I'll be a video for you'. Similarly, 'You can cash my check if you go down to the bank'. It's 'two for one for a limited time', and Byrne gets to the crux of the matter with the lines 'Love and money/Gettin' all mixed up'.

The original version of the song begins with someone – presumably Frantz – yelling 'One, two', then bursting into laughter before starting the count again and launching into the rollicking song. (Sadly, that rare moment of Talking Heads spontaneity has been cut from later versions.) The music has the feeling of four people playing together at the same time, with all the fun and freedom of a practice session at Frantz and Weymouth's Long Island City loft in Queens.

In the movie, the song appears as a music video, with the TV-obsessed character Swoozie Kurtz commenting on it. (Not surprisingly, 'Love For Sale' went into heavy rotation on MTV.) The video begins with silhouette shots of the band, but it's soon flooded with ad snippets for cameras, cars, vacuum cleaners, electric razors, soft drinks, airlines, toothpaste and hamburgers. (Byrne evidently went to great lengths to secure the rights to these images.)

Clearly, whatever prostitution is taking place here has to do with marketing and product placement. As the consumer goods continue to flash past (deodorant, lawn mowers, toilet paper, lipstick, candy, maple syrup, shaving cream, pizza), the band, each dressed in a bright primary color, become more and more enmeshed in the commercials, until finally they're all dipped in chocolate and wrapped in foil, with Weymouth suffering the ultimate indignity of having her head snapped off and eaten by an Olivia Newton-John look-alike. Who said Talking Heads couldn't laugh at themselves?

'Puzzlin' Evidence' (Byrne)
The movie version of 'Puzzlin' Evidence' features John Ingle (best known for his role as Edward Quartermaine in the soap opera *General Hospital*) playing a preacher sermonizing to his flock while an energetic choir backs him up. The film evokes hypocritical TV preachers of the time – like Jim Bakker and Jerry Falwell – which helps make sense of the otherwise contradictory lyric. But Ingle was no singer, and the song sounds much better in the Talking Heads version. A catchy rhythm soon morphs into Harrison's organ workout that makes a listener wish the musician had been given more opportunities to strut his stuff on previous albums. In his *Rolling Stone* review, Mark Coleman said the solo 'sweeps and hums like a cross between his Farfisa work on the Modern Lovers' first LP, and a Sunday morning gospel broadcast'. Then, a minute into the song, Byrne adopts the crazed-clergyman role himself, lambasting the media – 'You got *Time* and *Newsweek*/Well, they're the same to me' – while bragging about his own greatness: 'I got the power and glory/ And the money to buy it'. (He is the gun, we learn, and we are the bullet.)

As the title says, the evidence for his conspiracy theories is 'puzzlin'', as is his ultimate point. In one verse he's praising 'the little children' and 'the family', saying he wants to take them home with him. But in the next verse, he chastises his listeners: 'Well, I hope you're happy with what you've made/ In the land of the free and the home of the brave'. It's an epistemic free-for-all worthy of the sleaziest for-profit evangelist.

What ultimately drives the track is its gospel flavor, particularly the powerhouse performance by the Bert Cross Choir. Throughout the song, they respond to Byrne's perplexing statements with appropriate remarks of their own: 'Puzzlin'!' and 'Huh?' By the time we reach Harrison's inspired outro, even as the song builds to its crescendo, the choir feels more like an antagonist to the singer, and a collective voice of reason countering the preacher's frenzied, hypocritical sermon.

'Hey Now' (Byrne)
The St. Thomas Aquinas Elementary School Choir perform an abbreviated version of this song in the film. (They also add backing vocals to the Talking Heads version.) They appear suddenly and without explanation, moving across a building site – a group of boys and one little girl in pigtails and

glasses, all dressed in their school's Kelly green T-shirts. As they sing – with one of the boys leading a pet goat by a leash – they bang on scraps of lumber while another boy accents the beat on a hubcap. It's a lovely, strange scene and a celebration of the act of singing together.

Much of that raw energy comes across on the album. The two initial verses state a range of simple and comic desires: 'I want a bicycle/I want a popsicle/I want a space face/Buy me a cherry face now'. The final line of each verse is sung lower. The chorus, which consists of the title, is an irresistible sing-along, and there's an almost doo-wop feeling to the track.

The bridge, which changes key entirely, strains a bit towards the ethereal: 'Ohhh, when the light comes hit you in the eye/Heeyyy, gonna stop, gonna take you by surprise'. It's a nice moment of relief from the two chords bouncing back and forth in the rest of the song.

The guitar solo that follows has a Caribbean flavor, with the next two verses evoking a familial setting, the singer imploring 'your momma and daddy' to 'Leave those children alone'.

Another guitar solo – this one having a country-rock feel – follows the penultimate chorus, and then we get to the song's final statement, with the singer (accompanied by zydeco accordion) claiming powers that are regal ('I am the king of the world') if not godlike ('You can live to a hundred and ten/ If you listen to what I said'). Chorus repetitions take us to the final *cliché* three-accent ending. In truth, the song hasn't said much, but it nevertheless feels like a statement of purpose: sing, have fun and live your life to its fullest. Indeed, by the end of the trio of opening songs, devoted fans of the band hearing *True Stories* for the first time might have felt that the move towards Talking Heads-style Americana signaled in *Little Creatures* was now complete.

'Papa Legba' (Byrne)

Papa Lega is an important spirit in Haitian voodoo. Standing at the crossroads between the human and spiritual worlds, he is both guardian and messenger, someone who behooves those in need of favors on the earthly plane to beseech and placate.

In the role of Mr. Tucker (caretaker for Swoosie Kurtz's 'Lazy Woman'), Roebuck 'Pops' Staples also runs a side business in voodoo. His key role in the film is to act on behalf of Louis Fyne in his desperate quest for matrimony. In a later interview, Byrne lamented, 'I should never have sung it. That was for Pops to sing'. And you can see why he felt that way. Staples begins the song in a low recitation. But as it moves towards its climax – the camera showing us an altar packed with lit candles, skulls and snapshots of people who have sought his assistance – Staples comes to fully embody his character.

Despite the uphill battle of recording this song themselves, Talking Heads managed to bring their own Afro-Caribbean groove to the number. They received a huge helping hand from Brazilian percussionist Paulinho da Costa.

Talking Heads ... On Track

Indeed, the first half-minute is basically a solo performance, with shakers, rattles, drums, chimes and bells creating the necessary mood for Byrne to enter into Staples' role as intercessor to the Haitian spirit. The opening verse promises the person for whom the singer is working that they will be a 'magnet for money' and a 'magnet for love'. But verse two warns that getting to this point may not be easy: 'It might, hmm, hi, hi, hi, might rain fire'.

The Spanish pre-chorus 'Rompiendo la monotonía del tiempo' ('Breaking the monotony of time') is an appropriate sentiment for an appeal to Papa Legba, who can speak all languages. The singer also asks Papa Lega to 'open the gate ... to the city of camps' and to ride his horse in the night. The chorus benefits from Byrne's expert ability to turn just about any phrase he wrote into a hook. You want to join in, even if you have no idea who the title character is or why he's being petitioned.

'Wild Wild Life' (Byrne)
'Wild Wild Life' reached number 25 on the *Billboard* Hot 100, Talking Heads' third top 40 hit, after 'Take Me To The River' and 'Burning Down The House'. It was their final song to chart in America. MTV no doubt played an important role in the song's popularity. In the film, a cast of unlikely audience members lip-synch a few lines, then give way to the next person. In the video, some of the movie folks (John Goodman in particular) retain their screen time, though the MTV version gives much bigger roles to band members, including Harrison as Prince and Billy Idol and Frantz as a chubby, wide-eyed cowboy.

The lyric begins with classic Byrnian silliness:

I'm wearing fur pajamas
I ride a hot potato
It's tickling my fancy
Speak up, I can't hear you

Still, there's a narrative that wants to emerge. The singer is on a mountaintop with some news to tell us, apparently about the importance of inviting 'wild wild life' into our own short time on Earth.

The most consistent of the verses focuses on a businessman who has purchased some 'wild wild life' on his way to the stock exchange. A number of commentators have suggested that cocaine is the substance fueling all this frenetic activity, and that's certainly a possibility. But just as likely is the manic energy that has emanated from the band's live-wire leader – the man who ran laps around the stage and couldn't seem to stop moving in *Stop Making Sense*.

In addition to its party-on chorus, relentless drumming and cleverly positioned guitar parts, the song is notable for its memorable wordplay. There's the man in verse two 'sitting on a windowsill', though 'He spends his time behind closed doors'. Not to mention the hilariously reductive 'Peace of

95

mind?/It's a piece of cake'. And has there ever been as succinct and funny a summation of entropy and chaos theory as 'Things fall apart/It's scientific'? This nod to Yeats' 'The Second Coming' adds yet another layer of the allusiveness.

Talking Heads should have had dozens of hit singles, so it's disappointing that 'Love For Sale' and 'Radio Head' (the other two released in the US) – not to mention just about any other track on the album – never cracked the top 100. Nevertheless, while this may have been their last top 40 hit, their body of work overall has had a staying power over the decades that's only been matched by a handful of other artists.

'Radio Head' (Byrne)

The UK band Radiohead famously took their name from the first track on side two, this catchy Tex-Mex-inspired song. No doubt the key line for the young British rockers was 'Radio Head, the sound of a brand-new world'. And, indeed, they were to inspire a legion of fans equally devoted and dogged in their pursuit of every clue to their heroes' meanings and motivations.

Tito Larriva fronts the movie band called Los Globos in his role as Ramon. Esteban 'Steve' Jordan – the eye-patched, so-called Jimi Hendrix of the accordion – steals his scenes in the movie and also makes his mark on 'Radio Head'. Jordan's accordion is the dominant instrument on the album track, providing an element of fun and authenticity. Similarly, Paulinho da Costa's enthusiastic percussion-playing recalls some of the more exultant moments on *Speaking In Tongues*

The album's shortest song, 'Radio Head' tells the fairly coherent story of a person who is able to read the minds and 'wavelengths' of other people. The singer appears to have found someone special in this process. In the chorus, he tells us he's 'picking up something good'. There are relatively few non-sequiturs for a Talking Heads song, although Byrne practically whispers verse two's final line. Is he going to leave the Land of Noise? No's? Nose? Notes?

Regardless of any specific word, the song, like so many on this album, is ultimately a celebration of good feelings; an energetic and singable track, with Harrison and Weymouth providing exuberant backing vocals.

'Dream Operator' (Byrne)

The movie version of 'Dream Operator' is truly surreal. Sung by Annie McEnroe as Kay Culver, the uptight wife of the Varicorp executive, it takes place during a fashion show at the Virgil Mall. 'Shopping is a feeling', she tells her audience. However, it's not just any fashion show, but a chance for the actual show designer Adele Lutz (Byrne's girlfriend and later wife) to bring on the most preposterous outfits imaginable. There are matching bed sheets and pillow dresses, a family wearing what appear to be clothes made of AstroTurf, a quartet dressed as flowers and vegetables, a man dressed as a brick wall, and a woman dressed as an ionic Greek column. It's weird, of course, but also strangely touching – Kay Culver, like her models, is so sincere, and the audience of rubes is lapping it up. It's not just that they don't know any better – they are true innocents, appreciative of whatever is put before them.

However, McEnroe is far from being a great singer, and with Byrne at the microphone, the song takes on an added splendor and pathos. The four-and-a-half-minute track begins with more than a minute of instrumental buildup. A minor-key piano arpeggio is accompanied by bass, drums and guitar, sounding like a sad 1950s song. It all climaxes in a country-and-western-inflected guitar solo before Byrne launches into one of his more speculative lyrics.

The lines 'You must have been something/A real tiny kid' and 'I wish you were me/I wish I was you' hearken back to one of the great 1970s songs: Mott the Hoople's 'I Wish I Was Your Mother': 'I wish I could have seen you/ Could have been you as a child'. Ian Hunter's lyric and delivery made that song angrier and more desperate than 'Dream Operator', though a deep sense of longing is common to both tracks.

As the song title suggests, the narrative voice is enmeshed in the idea of the crossover between dreams and reality and their effect on romantic love. 'I've been waiting so long', Byrne sings, 'Now I am your dream'. Interestingly, it's the singer's beloved who is the actual dream operator. He is busy providing esoteric information like 'Every dream has a name' and 'Three angels above' look over 'the whole human race/They dream us to life/They dream me a face'. Meanwhile, the object of his devotion has 'dreamed it all/And this is your story'.

Of course, like so many Talking Heads songs, 'Dream Operator' is far more than the sum of its parts. Each time the chorus returns with its slightly varied lines, it feels like something important is being conveyed. It's partly the lovely music and Byrne's ardent singing, which on this album is probably as strong as it ever was with Talking Heads. When he reaches the bridge with its sardonic lines 'Shake it up, dream' and 'Fix it up, dream', he doesn't break character. And even when he sings in falsetto, the magic continues to the very end.

'People Like Us' (Byrne)
The climax of *True Stories*, the movie, is the town talent show held out in the middle of an empty field. Throughout the film, we see shots of crews preparing the large stage. And when night falls and the show begins, we get snippets (during the 'Papa Legba' segment) of some of the acts – dueling yo-yos, a woman dressed as a pat of butter while a giant puppet eats corn made of yellow balloons, a down-home ventriloquist act performed by two children, and aging line dancers in red, white and blue dresses. It's very odd stuff; all received rapturously by an adoring Virgil audience.

However, what the audience has been waiting for is the John Goodman/ Louis Fyne song with which he hopes to attract a life partner. Rubbing an

Indian-head good-luck charm given to him by Mr. Tucker, Louis takes to the stage with his band, The Country Bachelors. Dressed in a gray suit and cowboy hat, with a big grin and a bit of Elvis swagger, Louis delivers the highlight of Virgil's Sesquicentennial and finally snags his bride: the lazy rich woman who never gets out of bed. (Their wedding reception, naturally, is held in her bed.)

It's a tough scene to top, but the Talking Heads version is even better. Helped by Tommy Camfield on fiddle, Tommy Morrell on pedal steel and Paulinho da Costa on percussion, Talking Heads made an actual country record. Granted, 'People Like Us' never made the country chart (or any chart at all), but 'People Like Us', with its down-home lyrics and hummable melody, would sound good whether it was performed by Left Frizzell, Johnny Cash, Garth Brooks or Luke Bryan.

One question does arise: how ambiguous is the chorus? David Byrne, the bone-thin big-city avant-garde rock star, must surely look down on people who have grown 'as big as a house'. And yet, David Byrne, the autistic loner – so desperate to make connections with others and failing so often to do so – is surely the inspiration for the scene described in the second verse: 'I was called upon in the third-grade class/I gave my answer and it caused a fuss'. He tells us, 'I'm not the same as everyone else', and suddenly that fellow who back in 1978 wouldn't live in 'the big country' if you paid him seems to have found common ground with the *hoi polloi* he used to look down on.

The song's central argument that we shouldn't seek freedom and justice because it might interfere with our pursuit of love must surely be a joke. But this is the songwriter who years earlier said of 'Don't Worry About The Government', 'My voice gave an edge to it that wasn't quite what I was trying to say. I wanted it to sound sincere and genuine and sympathetic, and I think it sounds like I was being ironic'. Years later, he seems to have achieved his aim for the earlier song: his voice is under control, and he sounds more sincere and sympathetic than one would expect.

Concrete details bring 'People Like Us' to life. In addition to the embarrassing situation in the singer's third-grade class, we learn that he was born in 1950 (Byrne was born in 1952) and that his economically struggling father told him to 'Be proud of what you are'. And what better way of classifying the average American circa 1986 than as people 'Who will answer the telephone'. (How far we've come nearly 40 years later when practically no one will answer an unknown number on their phone.)

'City Of Dreams' (Byrne)
One of the greatest songs ever played over closing film credits, 'City Of Dreams' soars far beyond its source material in the film. On-screen, we meet again the girl of eight or nine whom we haven't seen since the movie's opening sequence. Barefoot in a white dress, she sings little songs and talks to herself as she dances and meanders up a straight dirt road, away from

the slowly rising camera, as the credits roll. In the distance, fields stretch to a horizon of blue sky.

On the album, a snare fill leads to a steady 4/4 rhythm and some firm piano pounding on three familiar chords. Soon, Byrne is inviting us into one of his most complex lyrics. Drawing on images seen early in the film, he provides us with a capsule history of the land around Virgil, Texas – from dinosaurs to Native Americans that the Spanish torture for gold and who are ultimately killed by white men, though their spirits 'haven't really gone'. Appropriately, the chorus tells us that while 'We live in the city of dreams', to get there and back, we must 'drive on this highway of fire'.

'City Of Dreams' is a song of persistence and sorrow. In verse two, we learn that those who settled in 'our favorite town' are from 'Germany and Europe and Southern USA', and we see that Byrne can't resist allowing a little sarcasm to seep in, as if Germany wasn't part of Europe. Nevertheless, verse three offers some qualified hope for a future that's been built on the tragedies of the past:

Underneath the concrete
The dream is still alive
A hundred million lifetimes
A world that never dies

The fairly simple chord structure underlies a gorgeous melody, which Byrne sings for all he's worth. Tommy Morrell is back on pedal steel, accenting the lyric and adding to the short solo. The keyboards round everything out, giving the track a real grandeur. If this had been the last song Talking Heads ever recorded, it would have been a worthy valediction.

Talking Heads ... On Track

Naked (1988)

Personnel:
David Byrne: vocals, guitar, keyboards, toy piano, slide guitar
Chris Frantz: drums, keyboard percussion
Jerry Harrison: piano, keyboards, guitar, slide guitar, tambourine, backing vocals
Tina Weymouth: bass, keyboards, organ, backing vocals
Kirsty MacColl: backing vocals ('(Nothing But) Flowers', 'Bill')
Johnny Marr: guitar ('Ruby Dear', '(Nothing But) Flowers', 'Mommy Daddy You And I', 'Cool Water')
Yves N'Djock: guitar ('Blind', 'Totally Nude', '(Nothing But) Flowers')
Eric Weissberg: pedal steel ('Totally Nude', 'Bill'), dobro ('The Democratic Circus')
Mory Kanté: kora ('Mr. Jones', 'The Facts Of Life')
Wally Badarou: keyboards ('Blind', 'The Facts Of Life')
Brice Wassy: percussion ('Ruby Dear', '(Nothing But) Flowers', 'The Facts Of Life', 'Big Daddy'
Abdou M'Boup: percussion, talking drum, congas, cowbell ('Blind', 'Mr. Jones', 'Totally Nude', '(Nothing But) Flowers')
Manolo Badrena: percussion, congas ('Mr. Jones', 'Mommy Daddy You And I')
Sydney Thiam: congas ('The Democratic Circus'); percussion ('Bill')
Moussa Cissokao: percussion ('Ruby Dear')
Nino Gioia: percussion ('The Facts Of Life')
Lenny Pickett, Steve Elson: saxophone ('Blind', 'Big Daddy')
Robin Eubanks: trombone ('Blind', 'Big Daddy', 'Mr. Jones')
Laurie Frink, Earl Gardner: trumpet ('Blind', 'Big Daddy')
Stan Harrison: alto saxophone ('Blind', 'Big Daddy')
Steve Gluzband, Jose Jerez, Charlie Sepulveda: trumpet ('Mr. Jones')
Al Acosta: tenor saxophone ('Mr. Jones')
Bobby Porcelli: alto saxophone ('Mr. Jones')
Steve Sacks: baritone saxophone ('Mr. Jones')
Dale Turk: bass trombone ('Mr. Jones')
Arthur Russell: cello ('Bill')
Philippe Servain: accordion ('Totally Nude')
James Fearnley: accordion ('Mommy Daddy You And I')
Phil Bodner: cor anglais ('Cool Water')
Don Brooks: harmonica ('Big Daddy')
Alex Haas: whistling ('Bill')
Producers: Steve Lillywhite, Talking Heads
Release date: 15 March 1988
Recorded: August-December 1987
Studios: Davout, Paris; Sigma Sound, New York City
Label: Fly/Sire
Running time: 52:17 (CD); 46:56 (LP)
Album charts: US: 19, UK: 3
Singles charts: 'Blind', UK: 59; '(Nothing But) Flowers', UK: 79

100

True Stories could well have been Talking Heads' last hurrah. After the album and movie were released, two long years passed, with Frantz, Weymouth and Harrison eager to tour. But Byrne was opposed to playing live, in part, he claimed, because he felt the *Stop Making Sense* tour could never be topped. Yet the other band members were restless. The thrill of co-writing the music that had kept Talking Heads together from *Fear Of Music* to *Remain In Light* and *Speaking In Tongues* was – after five years and two albums with Byrne as sole composer – a distant memory.

Byrne had been busy with other projects. He composed music for part of Robert Wilson's mammoth opera *The Civil Wars*, which Byrne called *The Knee Plays*. With musicians Ryuichi Sakamoto and Cong Su, Byrne contributed to the soundtrack for Bernardo Bertolucci's *The Last Emperor*. Their music was awarded an Oscar and a Grammy for Best Original Score. If making the cover of *Time* magazine didn't go to Byrne's head, surely his success in composing award-winning art music would.

Somehow (perhaps simply because of nostalgia), the others enticed Byrne back into the studio one last time. Frantz told Ron Hart in a 2018 *Billboard* interview:

Tina and I had a loft in Long Island City, where the band had rehearsed for many, many years. We recorded *Fear Of Music* there. We had lived there since 1976: we moved into that loft during the bicentennial weekend. And we all went back there and recorded these improvs on cassette. We were all very happy, including David, about the direction in which it was going. We made about 20 of these little musical snippets – not exactly songs, but more starting-off points, and took those with us to Paris.

Talking Heads' final album was recorded in Studio Davout, an old movie theatre on the outskirts of Paris. Weymouth, whose mother was French, was fluent in the language, and she felt especially at home in this setting. Harrison was excited, though he recalls that returning to the studio after a long time off was a stop-and-start process: 'Some days this process is better than others'. Nevertheless, they were all together again and eager to incorporate some of the many talented African musicians living in Paris into their new record. Byrne wrote of these players in *How Music Works* (among them guitarist Yves N'Djock, percussionist Abdou M'Boup and keyboardist Wally Badarou, who had played a significant role on *Speaking In Tongues*): 'They could adapt to styles outside of the traditions they had grown up with, and their response to our music was also entirely one of enthusiastic adaptation and accommodation'.

Talking Heads had not worked with a producer since Brian Eno back in 1980, but they agreed to ask Steve Lillywhite, who'd been involved with U2, Peter Gabriel and The Rolling Stones. Lillywhite remembered, 'I think what the band – Chris and Tina especially – wanted for *Naked* was to go back to a

Talking Heads ... On Track

time when they were all involved in the music, rather than just David coming in with a finished song. It was all done at the same time by all of them, and that was a change around for them from *Little Creatures* and *True Stories*, and I think gave them a lot of energy'.

Harrison wrote in the liner notes for the album's 2005 reissue: '*Naked* was an attempt to return to the recording techniques of *Remain In Light* and *Speaking In Tongues*: layered, poly-rhythmic tracks that interacted with each other to create moving textures as well as melodies and rhythms'.

As he'd done on earlier albums, Byrne sequestered himself with the session tapes and used nonsense placeholder phrases to get a sense of how words might match a song's rhythm until he could write more coherent lyrics. In *How Music Works*, he recalled coming up with the lyrics to '(Nothing But) Flowers' 'while driving around suburban Minneapolis'. He claimed, 'The only gear I needed to write lyrics was a cassette player to play the tracks for inspiration, another small one to record my lyric ideas, and a pad of paper to write them down on'.

According to David Bowman in *This Must Be The Place*, while 'Lillywhite didn't always agree with the band', he 'could tell right away what sections worked and what didn't. He made concrete suggestions and pushed things along. He wasn't moody like Eno. He was more conservative in the studio, but that had hidden blessings'. One of his concrete suggestions was to bring in guitarist Johnny Marr, who'd recently left The Smiths. Marr's playing gave an edge to songs like 'Ruby Dear' and '(Nothing But) Flowers'. Lillywhite also found a place for his wife, Kirsty MacColl, as a background vocalist. In Frantz's words, MacColl 'sang like an angel, and she could effortlessly layer harmonies the way The Beach Boys did'.

Frantz insists that the group had always planned to have a monkey on the cover, though he says Weymouth wanted to call the album *The Higher The Monkey Climb, The More He Expose*: a Jamaican saying that they found amusing. In a *Billboard* interview, Frantz says, 'It was our designer Tibor Kalman who had come across a painter (Paula Wright) on 42nd St who did animal portraits ... So he said, 'Why don't we have her do a very formal portrait of a chimpanzee?' and she did it. It was super inexpensive, much cheaper than having Robert Mapplethorpe take your picture'. The chimp on the cover is painted against a red backdrop and holds a violet in his right hand. His mouth is partly open, as though he has just finished speaking or is about to. The picture is centered in an elaborate gilded wooden frame, which emphasizes the absurdity of the main image. The back cover is a photograph of a pond or stream in a jungle setting, presumably a place where the front cover subject would feel at home.

Released in March 1988, the album initially did fairly well, though sales dropped off quickly, which Frantz and Weymouth attributed to Byrne's refusal to go on tour. Giving the album a B+, Robert Christgau wrote, 'Where Paul Simon appropriated African musicians, David Byrne just hires them, for better

102

and worse – this is T. Heads funk heavy on the horns, which aren't fussy or obtrusive because Byrne knew where to get fresh ones'.

Anthony DeCurtis concluded his *Rolling Stone* review as follows:

The Chinese proverb 'If there is no tiger in the mountains, the monkey will be king' is printed on the jacket of *Naked*, and a framed portrait of a monkey adorns the cover. 'The human race consists of some pretty cool people', *Naked* seems to be saying, but it's got a very destructive monkey on its back. Human survival is not guaranteed. With humor and good-heartedness, hope and fear, Talking Heads contemplate a world on the eve of destruction on this important record and leave wide open the question of what the dawn will bring.

The dawn, alas, brought no more new Talking Heads albums. While the official breakup was still several years away, and a handful of new songs were cobbled together from previously recorded music, this was the band's swan song, in all its contradictions and imperfections.

In the *Billboard* interview, Frantz remembered:

We had a really good time making this record, especially when we were in Paris. We hadn't done anything in a while, and things went so well that it gave the rest of the band hope that there would be more. And why shouldn't there have been? We were, in my opinion, reaching another level in our sound. Sadly, it didn't work out that way, but it was fun while it lasted.

Fun, indeed. *Ave atque vale*, Talking Heads.

'Blind' (Lyrics: Byrne; Music: Byrne, Frantz, Harrison, Weymouth)
In the liner notes for *Once In A Lifetime: The Best Of Talking Heads*, Weymouth presents a rather unflattering portrait of Byrne composing 'Blind' in the studio:

David uncharacteristically wore a suit to his vocal session, as well as a pair of clear-glass black horn rims. He looked so small as he sat at a large office desk ... His hands lay palms down, fingers splayed to either side of the paper, and he never moved them except during the instrumental section to reach for a glass of water that stood in the shadows to one side ... The only lyric that came from that improvisation was the chorus in which he sings, 'Blahnd, blahnd, blahnd'. His head moved like a muppet, and we all watched, fascinated as if he were a bug on a pin under a microscope.

To borrow from Austin Powers: *Ouch, Tina, very ouch.*

That one session may have only resulted in the chorus, but Byrne came up with a politically charged and deeply intriguing lyric that, for him, feels almost like a narrative. (Unfortunately, the video undercuts the lyric's seriousness with

Talking Heads ... *On Track*

a comical talking and spitting wrench, vaguely reminiscent of the goose-stepping hammers in Pink Floyd's film *The Wall*.) Moreover, the riffs from the Long Island City jams that evolved into 'Blind' are among the catchiest in the Talking Heads repertoire.

The song begins with a horn section (along with an annoying and repetitive guitar note) that demands your attention even before Weymouth steps in with a funky bass line, and Byrne launches into lines that could have been written by American novelist Don Delillo: 'Signs/Signs are lost/Signs disappeared ... Somebody got busted/Got a face of stone and a ghostwritten biography'. Gradually, a portrait emerges of a person accused of being a terrorist who was 'Torn all apart/All in the name of democracy'. However, by the end of the first verse, we're still unsure of the man's crime or innocence: 'No one ever said that he was involved with thieves'. Then comes the unforgettable chorus. A couple of words of introduction ('And they're' or 'And I'm') and the title is sung 14 times, all in that stylized pronunciation Weymouth mocked as 'Blahnd'. Once again, Byrne's ability to make a hook out of the simplest materials is on full display.

Throughout the song, Byrne's voice sounds strained, as if this is the 15th take and he's determined to get it right. That urgency surges into a passage that will be repeated near the end of the song. Clearly winking at the lack of harmonic movement in 'Blind', Byrne jests, 'No sense of harmony' and 'Don't mention harmony/Say, What is it? What is it?' After this apparent misdirection, the song gets to its crux – a man, presumably the character from the long opening verse, 'was shot down in the night/People ride by/But his body's still alive'. And suddenly, there is a new character: 'The girl in the window' looking down on the scene. 'What has she done?' the singer wonders, as the girl cries out "I don't want to die!".'

An ambiguous four lines with the singer demanding 'What the hell is going on?' precede the repetition of the 'no sense of harmony' and 'shot down in the night' section. In the final chorus, we get 28 statements of the word 'blind' until it almost becomes a mantra.

As the outro horns kick in, we can truly appreciate the charts of tenor saxophonist Lenny Pickett, who is making a return from *Little Creatures*. We also register other sounds that have been repeating incessantly throughout the song: Frantz's drums, of course, but also Abdou M'Boup on talking drum, congas and cowbell, Wally Badarou on keyboard congas, Weymouth's deceptively simple bass line, and Harrison's riff on the French piano, which occasionally breaks through the wall of sound like a prisoner tunneling out of jail. One final ripping solo from Yves N'Djock brings the song just about to the end, and a big horn flourish takes it out.

'Mr. Jones' (Lyrics: Byrne; Music: Byrne, Frantz, Harrison, Weymouth)
To open this track, Abdou M'Boup teams up with Manolo Badrena, the percussionist on Weather Report's landmark 1977 album *Heavy Weather*.

Percussion is soon joined by Mory Kanté playing a delicate figure on the kora, a West African instrument that sounds somewhat like a lute. It's a mysterious and subtle sound, interrupted 30 seconds in by the unstoppable *Naked* horn section.

Suddenly, we're in an entirely different world as Byrne sings about Mr. Jones, a man who will 'Put a wiggle in your stride' now that he's changed into his 'ventilated slacks'. Then this gentleman with 'tight pants' and 'curly hair' is on the dance floor, drinking cold beer and moonshine and doing something unspecified with 'Handi-wipes'.

Mr. Jones originally appeared in Bob Dylan's 1965 song 'Ballad Of A Thin Man', where the protagonist is told 'Something is happening here and you don't know what it is/Do you, Mr. Jones?' (John Lennon alludes to the character in The Beatles' 1968 song 'Yer Blues': 'Feel so suicidal, just like Dylan's Mr. Jones'.) On the podcast *This Must Be Talking Heads*, Byrne explains that his protagonist was 'the same guy from Bob Dylan's Mr. Jones, but now he's having a good time. He's at the hotel. There's a convention going. He's with his friends. He's not an outsider anymore'. Byrne's Mr. Jones is far more multidimensional than Dylan's original version, a sad sack who tries so hard but still doesn't understand anything. Sure, the Mr. Jones on *Naked* may have some clothing malfunctions ('Now his pants are falling down'), but 'He is not so square'; 'It's his lucky day'. Indeed, he parties not only with salesmen and conventioneers but with 'Some rock stars with tambourines/Short skirts and skinny legs'. Weirdly, these rock stars are 'Selling Bibles and real estate'. Things get even weirder in the final verse when we learn there is a 'Jones Gang down at the bar'. What have they done? It's not clear, but whatever it is, 'They've gone too far'. The singer insinuates that it's probably best to avoid Mr. Jones's hotel room, where 'party favors' are being distributed.

This wacky lyric is accompanied by a swinging Latin-jazz big band made up of members of an ensemble Byrne had heard playing with Celia Cruz and Ray Baretto in New York. Byrne asked for an arrangement in the style of the Cuban pianist/composer Perez Prado (who was partly responsible for popularizing the mambo in the 1950s), and trumpeter Angel Fernandez delivered the chart. The jazz band is such a big and irresistible part of the track's sound that, at times, the other three Talking Heads members practically disappear. Indeed, 'Mr Jones' would not be out of place on Byrne's next solo album, *Rei Momo*. One wonders if when they heard the final mix, Frantz, Weymouth and Harrison suspected that the end was nigh.

'Totally Nude' (Lyrics: Byrne; Music: Byrne, Frantz, Harrison, Weymouth)
Yves N'Djock leads the way into and through 'Totally Nude' with a steel guitar that has echoes of soukous and country-and-western music. It's a lazy, lovely sound, at odds, yet somehow in harmony with Adou M'Boup's brisk, unrelenting percussion. As the song proceeds, in the background you can just hear Phillipe Servain's accordion helping to carry the tune.

'Totally Nude' has a distinctly more mellow musical vibe than the previous two songs, and the lyric matches the music, with Byrne's wry sense of humor on full display: 'Totally naked, Baby/Totally nude/'Cause if I want to, who's gonna stop me?' Throughout, Byrne champions nudity in a way that's playful yet feels sincere. He tells us he's 'a nature boy locked up inside' and he wants to follow a 'Nature boy, nature man' to 'a life that's undiscovered'. The fact that the album is titled *Naked* makes 'Totally Nude' a key track, with the singer's declaration toward the end, 'We don't need clothes and we don't need money' being a kind of statement of the album's purpose: Live free from social constraints; be yourself. The line that follows – 'So civilized' – suggests that the most civilized course of action is the one that's least beholden to current ideas of civilization.

Just before those lines, there is what appears to be a sly reference to Bob and Judy, the heroes of 'Found A Job' on *More Songs About Buildings And Food*. In 'Totally Nude', we hear about a polka party for Bob and Martha. Possibly, Bob has found a new mate. It's an apt narrative arc from 1978 to 1988. The earlier characters' lives were devoted to making TV shows, while Bob and his current partner dance the polka in the nude with the nature boy narrator. In 'Found A Job', Byrne admonished his listeners, 'If your work isn't what you love/Then something isn't right'. In 'Totally Nude', the singer and his crew appear to have taken that advice to heart.

'Ruby Dear' (Lyrics: Byrne: Byrne, Frantz, Harrison, Weymouth)
The jazz standard 'Ruby, My Dear', written by Thelonious Monk in 1945, sounds nothing like 'Ruby Dear'. Rather than a bluesy late-night solo piano, the track opens with a wall of drumming that increases in volume until Byrne sings "Round and 'round and we won't let go/ And where we stop no one knows'. Nevertheless, there is something almost Monk-inspired about the song's investigation of a noir-ish world gone wrong: a place of broken records, dirty rivers, angels and prostitutes.

As Jon Parles wrote in his 1988 *New York Times* review of *Naked*, "Ruby Dear', with its insistent Bo Diddley beat behind a curtain of guitars, forecasts the opposite (of 'Totally Nude'): an ecological breakdown'. The juxtaposition of the songs is striking and unsettling. Clearly we listeners cannot trust in the idyllic world Byrne has just finished conjuring up for us.

In the middle of the song, there is a moment when Byrne sounds as though he's retained at least some hope: 'I still like the ocean/Down by the sea'. But he follows that line with 'They left that door wide open/It tempted me', implying that the sea was simply a place for him to exit the Hellish life he was living.

The Ruby character is enigmatic. She seems to be primarily a figure the singer can address his own thoughts to, first about 'what everyone is saying', then about late-night radio and the fact that the river has dried up. The fourth and final time the singer mentions Ruby, she is hounding him from the bedroom to the kitchen. Granted, this is a song, not a short story, but the singer offers some tantalizing clues around which to build a picture of their relationship.

'Ruby Dear' also marks the album's first appearance by guitarist Johnny Marr, and he provides a suitably Smiths-like accompaniment, giving the song's few chords a chiming, foreboding delivery. His presence is particularly notable in the final verse, as Byrne describes a world of bonfires on the streets and 'rotten air'. Never less than driving, thanks to Moussa Cissokao on oil drums and Brice Wassy on maracas and leg-seed pods, the track ends abruptly, leaving us uncomfortable, wondering what in the world will come next.

'(Nothing But) Flowers' (Lyrics: Byrne; Music: Byrne, Frantz, Harrison, Weymouth)

What comes next is one of the glories of the Talking Heads songbook. 'Totally Nude' was full of boundless optimism, which 'Ruby Dear' ruthlessly undermined. '(Nothing But) Flowers' takes the Edenic vision of the former song and places it after civilization's collapse. If the vicissitudes of 'Ruby Dear' have taken place, the singer has forgotten all about them. Instead, he's so nostalgic for the bad old days that he can't enjoy his new paradise.

The music begins with M'Boup on congas and Wassy on the shaker. The bass part slides up and down as Weymouth waits to zero in on her groove. Yves N'Djock's guitar-playing – as ever, a lodestar for the other musicians – dances and celebrates throughout the song. Johnny Marr's 12-string electric adds another layer of far-out charm, as do the background vocals of Kirsty MacColl, the unforgettable second voice heard on The Pogues' 'Fairytale Of New York'.

Initially, we may believe Byrne's tongue is very much in his cheek. After describing a 'Garden of Eden' with waterfalls and 'birds in the trees', he tells us, 'From the age of dinosaurs, cars have run on gasoline'. In the next line, he longs for those gas-guzzling cars: 'Where? Where have they gone?' The singer misses the world of the late 1980s – a place of parking lots transformed in the future into peaceful oases, where Pizza Huts are now 'covered with daisies'. 'If this is paradise', he tells us, 'I wish I had a lawnmower'. 'You've got it, you've got it', Byrne sings in a slightly smarmy voice after many of the descriptions of life in the brave new world, either ridiculing the old world, the new, or both.

And yet, the loveliness of the tune carries us beyond the obvious ironies. Just before the bridge, Harrison enters with a few bars on the Hammond organ that are uplifting and a tad melancholy. Then Byrne acknowledges, 'Years ago, I was an angry young man'. He used to pretend to be a billboard (apparently one of his RISD art projects), but now, in this land of tranquil vegetation, he's become someone else. Sure, he may 'miss the honky tonks/ Dairy Queens and 7-Elevens', and he may feel that he 'can't get used to this lifestyle', but the joyful music and (mostly) ebullient singing tell another story. This new version of our singer is a better and, ultimately, happier man.

One final note – Just as 'Totally Nude' seems to reference 'Found A Job', '(Nothing But) Flowers' appears to give a nod to 'Animals' from *Fear Of Music*. In that song, 'living on nuts and berries' is dismissively associated with animals who don't need money, don't worry, are hairy and in general are 'making a fool of us'. Now Byrne admits, 'We used to microwave'. However, in the future, people, like animals, 'just eat nuts and berries'. Similar to the late-era Beatles ('The walrus was Paul'), late-era Talking Heads have created their own self-referential universe.

'The Democratic Circus' (Lyrics: Byrne; Music: Byrne, Frantz, Harrison, Weymouth)

CD sales overtook those of vinyl in 1987, and by the following year, the idea of the two-sided record or cassette began to seem less relevant. Nevertheless, *Naked* clearly has the feel of an A-side (upbeat songs, the hits) and a B-side (stranger, more experimental songs).

'The Democratic Circus' certainly shifts the mood. Rather than the feel-good dance party of '(Nothing But) Flowers', we now have a muted rhythm, with Eric Weissberg on dobro, its strings resonating with the feel of the Great Depression. For a full minute, the track sounds like it will be a country blues. But once Byrne begins singing, we discover the track will indeed be a comparison between democracy circa 1988 and an actual circus.

One of Byrne's strengths as a lyricist is his ambivalence. Obfuscation, misdirection, contradiction and sometimes outright silliness had been hallmarks of his lyrics. Alas, despite the inevitable ducks and feints, 'The Democratic Circus' is a pretty straightforward teardown of big-party politics. In verse one, we learn that the circus is actually populated by Secret Service types wielding 'walkie-talkies' as they usher their elected charges through the crowds in Cadillacs.

The circus – to use a bit of literary terminology – is the vehicle being used to describe the tenor of politics. It's a pretty worn metaphor, though Byrne does his best to inject some life into it. We have the expected sideshows and the Tunnel of Love and Ferris Wheel, but the singer adds a bit of sinister, Bradbury-esque mystery (*Something Wicked This Way Comes*) to the speaker and his friends' encounter with the ringmaster. After the ringmaster calls their names, they will be 'the first ones to go to sleep/Stealing all our dreams/ Dreams for sale/They'll sell 'em back to you'.

Harrison's entrance with a growling electric guitar about halfway through adds some tension and menace to the second half, emphasizing the irony of lines like 'How we all laughed/We split our sides'. The final half-minute of the outro on the dobro is a nice touch. But lyrically, the analogy never quite rises to true Byrnian heights. Instead, we are left with that *rara avis* in the Talking Heads canon: a song that's a little too obvious.

'The Facts Of Life' (Lyrics: Byrne; Music: Byrne, Frantz, Harrison, Weymouth)

Naked is an album of contrasts, and the biggest one comes when we hit the second song on side two. Having been lulled into a mellow, if melancholy mood by Eric Weissberg's dobro-playing on the previous track, we are suddenly faced with an entirely different kind of music.

The various synthesizers on 'The Facts Of Life' offer an idea of the song's sonic palette: Weymouth: Machine; Harrison: Scream, Bass, Flute; Wally Badarou: Sonar, Pedal steel. For added texture, Mory Kanté is back on the kora, and Brice Wassy plays the bells and spoons. Frantz's drumming is appropriately mechanical, resulting in an overwhelming and repetitive noise, even by the standards of this album. You can imagine the music working well as the soundtrack to Fritz Lang's *Metropolis* (1927).

If any track could be said to be the inspiration for the cover image of the chimpanzee holding a flower, it's 'The Facts Of Life'. Monkeys and chimps are mentioned five times in the song. But the opening verse seems ambiguous at best about our simian cousins:

Monkey see and monkey do
Making babies, eating food
Smelly things, pubic hair
Words of love in the air

Less than a minute later, after singing the title, Byrne, in his curveball way, addresses sexual desire: 'Boys 'n' girls and automation/Chromosomes, designer jeans/And chimpanzees and human beings'.

Towards the end, Byrne sings in a falsetto that would make Mick Jagger proud: 'So much sex 'n' violence must be a bad design/We're stupid to be fighting' – then, switching to a deeper voice – 'Every night'. Clearly, in Byrne's mind, the facts of life don't only refer to sex but to our chromosomes and 'bad design'. In the third reference to simians, we see his distrust of biological reproduction (perhaps a middle finger to his three bandmates with children): 'The girls and boys combine like monkeys in the zoo'.

After a short display of industrial-sounding synth playing, the song grows mellow for what might be called a late bridge. Some of the more obnoxious synthesizer sounds drop out, replaced by slide guitar, and Byrne croons, 'People fall in love like in fairy tales'. But he immediately destabilizes any romance that statement might have evoked: 'I'm not sure I like what they can do/I'm afraid God has no master plan/He only takes what he can use'. In the next verse, he tells us that life is simply a 'factory', and we live a 'factory life'.

The fourth and fifth references to simians, sung again in falsetto, are found in the final verse:

Someday we'll live on Venus
Men will walk on Mars
But we'll still be monkeys deep down inside
If chimpanzees are smart
Then we will close our eyes
And let our instincts guide us

It's hardly a ringing endorsement for the future of the higher primates, and the outro, more than a minute long in the more mellow vein of kora and guitar, allows us plenty of time to reflect on Byrne's rather dire assessment of love, sexuality and procreation.

'Mommy Daddy You And I' (Lyrics: Byrne; Music: Byrne, Frantz, Harrison, Weymouth)
This song begins with a bass riff that, for an instant, feels as though it might resolve into 'Psycho Killer'. But it doesn't. Instead, Johnny Marr plays with the whammy bar while James Fearnley fingers a nervous chord on the accordion. It sounds like we are in for another acoustic jam *à la* 'The Democratic Circus', and that's what we essentially get. Soon, the tempo picks up, with Frantz's drumming and Manolo Badrena's percussion accentuating the feel of the central experience: 'A-riding on a bus/The high and the low/Mommy, Daddy, you and I'.

The song draws on at least one autobiographical fact: Byrne spent the longest stretch of his childhood in the suburbs of Baltimore. But the family in the song is essentially running away from town on a bus that's so crowded they have to stand until they have blisters on their feet. Byrne's father was an electrical engineer for a major corporation, so there was never a time when the Byrne family was forced to go north 'wearing our grandfather's clothes/'Cause we hear that up north it gets cold'.

If we remove the biographical David Byrne from the song – which is nearly always a good idea on a Talking Heads record – what we have is the story of a family in flight, a classic immigrant tale about those who must start over at a moment's notice, 'Making changes day by day', with only the clothes on their back. By singing in the first person, Byrne embodies the experience, which he makes even more real through the use of well-observed details like 'Sleeping on my daddy's shoulder' and 'Drinking from a paper cup'.

'Mommy Daddy You And I' might have been more at home on *Little Creatures*, but *Naked* is so diverse in its musical offerings that the track doesn't stand out as an anomaly. Ultimately, it is a song about facing and surmounting challenges, an expression of optimism, though it is the last glimpse of hope that we find on this album.

'Big Daddy' (Lyrics: Byrne; Music: Byrne, Frantz, Harrison, Weymouth)
Family reemerges as a topic here, but this unit is not as cohesive as the one on the previous track. The title immediately recalls Big Daddy, the patriarch

Talking Heads ... On Track

of Tennessee Williams's 1955 play *Cat On A Hot Tin Roof*. In that work, Big Daddy is dying of cancer, though his doctor won't tell him or his wife Big Mama the truth about his condition. Big Daddy presides over a family that includes his closeted gay, alcoholic son Brick, Brick's wildly ambitious daughter-in-law Maggie, Brick's scheming and greedy brother Gooper, and Gooper's conniving wife Mae. It's a real Southern Gothic shit show.

However, *Cat On A Hot Tin Roof* has nothing on the story suggested by this lyric. Here, we also have a powerful head of the household, but he's even creepier than the Tennessee Williams version. This Big Daddy uses his wealth to secure sex from a variety of (presumably) young girls, those with 'tiny tears/Just like a Barbie doll': the sort of individual who 'likes to shop at Sears and visit shopping malls'. Before verse one is over, we learn that the girl with the Barbie doll tears is now 'a Big Mama' who is advised to 'Tell Poppa' and then 'Cry, cry, cry, cry'.

This sordid tale of woe is introduced with the oversized horn sound of 'Blind' and 'Mr. Jones', this time arranged by Lenny Pickett and Jerry Harrison. The big, punchy bursts of rhythm from saxophone, trumpets, trombone and flugelhorn all but drown out the lyric's simmering pathos. And when all-star harmonica hero Don Brooks jumps in on blues harp, listeners can be excused for wanting to leap up from their seats rather than mull over the sad fate of Big Daddy's victims.

Against Weymouth's descending bass line, Byrne tells how Big Daddy's latest object of desire 'is gonna bite' on his bait of 'shiny things like jewels and gold'. It's never really clear who the other characters are, though whatever their tangled relationships may be, it's a creepy, corrupt world, one shot-through with money and violence: 'The velvet lies sing softly/Each with a golden spoon'. There is, however, the threat that the title character's misdeeds will catch up with him: 'And Big Daddy laughed/And Big Daddy smiled/One fine day she'll explode/Who's laughing now?'

'Bill' (Lyrics: Byrne; Music: Byrne, Frantz, Harrison, Weymouth)
'Bill' appeared on the CD and cassette versions of the album but was kept off the vinyl. And what did the vinyl listeners miss? The answer is probably the most discomfiting song in the Talking Heads catalog.

In *Once In A Lifetime*, Ian Gittins quotes Byrne telling interviewers: 'My Randy Newman tendencies surfaced in a song about a child molester'. As Gittins notes, 'Like Nabokov in *Lolita*, (Byrne) writes as if the offender is blameless and as much a victim as the girl', with the 'doomed liaison set to end in a grisly suicide pact, as Bill buys a gun and his underage love prepares to die'. That's essentially the story, although it's made all the creepier by the lyric: 'Bill was a man who grew too big' and found the girls always running away from him. In a comment heavy with foreboding, Byrne sings, 'When everybody laughs at you/It can be humiliating'. Then things take a dive: 'Billy likes a cute little girl/They are lovers, we can tell/Kisses on the mouth/

111

Holding hands and all'. That 'and all' speaks volumes, with the next verse making the two sound like high-school lovers: 'Sneaking off together/Running to the woods/Swimming in the river'.

Musically, 'Bill' is among the acoustic songs, with Harrison playing slide guitar, Weissberg on pedal steel, Kirsty MacColl on background vocals, and avant-garde cellist Arthur Russell adding a suitably eerie part. Frantz and Weymouth provide an uncomfortable start/stop rhythm, with Harrison's synth marimba further emphasizing the sinister subject matter.

'Cool Water' (Lyrics: Byrne; Music: Byrne, Frantz, Harrison, Weymouth) On this, the final official song on the final Talking Heads studio album, they regroup into something closer to a four-piece band, though Johnny Marr's delicate guitar and Phil Bodner's cor anglais solo (the instrument featured so memorably in Dvorak's ninth symphony) add an air of mystery and melancholy to a song about the end of the world. Rather than the avant-garde dance band that emerged from CBGB in 1976/1977, this version of Talking Heads could almost be a darker, late-1980s version of Fairport Convention or Pentangle.

'Day by day/Whistle while you work', the singer advises a group of people whom we surmise (as Frantz's martial snare rhythm gradually rises in volume) to be soldiers defending humanity against an alien takeover. We are 'Bags of bone and skin', Byrne tells us, 'But their skin is the same as yours/They can sit at the table too/The same blood as you and me'. After a brief acoustic interlude, things get even more gloomy for the people of Earth, with an alien sleeping in the singer's bed while 'Priests pass by/Worms crawl in'. Granted, 'Some have fallen down/And blood spilled on the ground', but, essentially, 'The work is over now/And rest will be at hand', presumably because humans will have been outnumbered and outfought.

Of course, the lyric is by David Byrne, so listeners have to stitch the narrative together to create a story that may or may not reflect the singer's actual intention. In that regard, 'Cool Water' is a typical Talking Heads song – intriguing, ambivalent, worth re-hearing, but ultimately a work of art that refuses to kowtow to the masses. If the band had always had one hand in the air waving to the idiosyncratic rhythm it had created, the other hand was slyly thumbing its nose at the unconverted.

Studio Songs Not Included On The Original Studio Albums

In *This Must Be The Place*, David Bowman says that in the early 1990s, the 'CD market was hungry for compilation packages that contained outtakes, alternate cuts, new songs, forgotten songs, covered songs'. He points out that in 1990, Bob Dylan released a 3-CD set of such songs, but 'Unfortunately, Talking Heads was not as prolific as Mr. Zimmerman'. When putting together the songs for *Popular Favorites 1976-1992: Sand In The Vaseline,* the band 'unearthed only four early tracks that predated *Talking Heads: 77*. Those tracks were 'Sugar On My Tongue, 'I Want To Live', 'Love → Building On Fire' and 'I Wish You Wouldn't Say That'. A fifth fully completed early song, 'I Feel It In My Heart', was included on the 2005 expanded edition of *Talking Heads: 77.*

For *Popular Favorites*, the band also 'unspooled four unused instrumental tapes from various *Remain In Light, Speaking In Tongues* and *Naked* sessions, and used these to create four new songs'. Very different in tone from the 1970s-era songs but very much in keeping with the sound of late-Talking Heads, the four newly minted tracks were 'Sax And Violins', 'Gangster Of Love', 'Lifetime Piling Up' and 'Popsicle'. Because the music was already recorded for earlier projects, and Byrne simply added lyrics and vocals, it's a stretch to call these songs collaborations, though the band is certainly playing at a high level behind Byrne's singing.

One final track, 'In Asking Land' – a reworking of 'Carnival Eyes', a song from Byrne's solo album *Rei Momo* – was originally created in the *Naked* sessions and is included below.

This section excludes unfinished outtakes like 'Dancing For Money' on the 2005 expanded version of *Fear Of Music* and experimental tracks that can't really be classified as songs in the traditional sense, such as the instrumental jams not used on the studio version of *Remain In Light* ('Fela's Riff', Double Groove' etc.) Hardcore fans may also miss discussion of alternative takes of studio songs or gimmicky shorts such as Byrne's solo acoustic version of one verse and one chorus of Nancy Sinatra's 'These Boots Are Made For Walkin',' which can be found on the compilation *Bonus Rarities & Outtakes*. However, we will leave the analysis of these extras to the many websites devoted to picking through every last scrap of the band's recorded material and concentrate on fully completed tracks.

Coverage of the following songs is roughly chronological, with post-*Naked* songs discussed in the order the musical materials were created and/or the order in which they were released.

'Sugar On My Tongue' (1975) (Byrne)
This unreleased demo, recorded directly to two-track and produced by Mark Spector, is too *pop* for the edgy *Talking Heads: 77*, but it is quite successful in its own right.

Talking Heads ... On Track

It begins with a little drama of picked strings, Frantz striking the drums once every fourth beat, four times through, before Weymouth joins in on bass, which often in these early recordings sounds as though it wasn't strung quite as tightly as it could have been. Nevertheless, she settles right into one of her classic minimalist patterns, and the song is off with two mournful 'Oh-oh-oh's from Byrne.

The narrator tells of a neighbor who can fill his cup by putting sugar on his tongue, as he wonders, 'Is she gonna gimme, gimme, gimme some?' 'Sugar' seems to cry out as a metaphor. Is the singer's neighbor placing a sugar cube containing LSD on his tongue? Or is sugar simply a synonym for sex? Both interpretations are possible, but considering the naivete displayed by so many of Byrne's narrators, the sugar could well be just a heaping spoonful of C & H.

It doesn't much matter, of course, as the joy is in singing the handful of lines, and the song's melody – mostly carried by two chords – is sweetly irresistible. In the bridge, the singer tells us he's 'been waiting years and years', and strangely, though in some ways suitably for a lyricist obsessed with the approval of his companions, his friends will be there to ask him, 'Is this the time that we're gonna see her/Put the sugar on your tongue?'

Whatever is happening, once the sugar hits the singer's tongue, or even when he just *thinks* of the experience, it practically wipes him out, with the final half-minute of this two-and-a-half-minute song devoted to wordless vocalizing that sounds both ecstatic and painful.

'I Want To Live' (1976) (Byrne)

Like 'Sugar On My Tongue', 'I Want To Live' was produced by Mark Spector with the three-piece band, and it has a similarly pleasing raw sound, with Weymouth's bass even more jagged than on the earlier song. David Bowman notes in *This Must Be The Place* that although the two songs 'would be lost for many years', they 'reveal how much Tina carried the band, provided the drive and the diversity'.

Byrne works his usual magic, pulling a melody out of the simplest material (five chords in this case), but the lyric is fairly uninspired. He wants to live, but the person he's been with is gone. He had some friends (there they are again), but he wants some more. 'Deeper feelings recur again and again and again and again' sounds like it's straight from his notebook.

However, in the final verse, four of Byrne's most poetic lines appear:

I want to live
To see the Earth turn one more time
I want to live
To feel a hand that isn't mine

It's a lovely moment, and even if (or perhaps because) his voice wavers as he holds the final note on 'time' and 'mine', the emotion feels genuine. With

114

its lo-fi production, 'I Want To Live' sounds very much like an early song, but even here, Byrne has transcended the bounds of the nascent songwriter.

'Love → Building On Fire' (1977) (Byrne)

This song was Talking Heads' first single, and while it is memorable, the band decided it was too different from the other material to be included on *Talking Heads: 77*.

The title catches one's attention even before the first note. What's with the arrow? Is it a direction sign? A *mis*direction sign? A mark of equivalency? None of the above, perhaps, or a little of each. (The title said aloud is usually 'Love goes to (a) building on fire'.) Like so many of Byrne's compositions, this is an anti-love song, the key lines in the first verse being 'I can't compare love when it's not love'. 'It's not love' is repeated two more times before we enter the linguistic funhouse of the chorus: 'Which is my face?/Which is a building?/Which is on fire?/On fire'.

Byrne seems to be defining through negation: the thing that is *not* love is his face, a building, and something on fire. Yet, like the old Intro to Philosophy game, 'Think of anything but an elephant' – love, faces, buildings and fires appear whether we want them to or not. Upon reflection, the ambiguous arrow feels just right for the song.

In the first 30 seconds, the rhythm guitar sounds almost like a synthesized harpsichord (Harrison had not yet joined the band), but when Byrne begins to sing about fire, the sound becomes richer, the drums and bass steadier and more present as he repeats the first verse and chorus. After the second time through, horns enter. The arrangement is credited to Brad Baker and Lance Quinn, although, in *Remain In Love,* Frantz sums up this unusual (for early-Talking Heads) instrumentation as follows: 'Overnight, a cat named Brad Baker wrote a horn arrangement that was performed by saxophonists Lew Del Gatto and 'Blue Lou' Marini. Lou Marini also played trumpet. I was hoping this would make us sound more like a Stax band, but no. We still sounded like Talking Heads'.

While 'Love → Building On Fire' might not resemble an outtake from the Stax catalog, it provides an intriguing hint of things to come much later on *Naked* and in Byrne's solo career, as well as a tantalizing glimpse of what the band might have sounded like had they pursued this direction in their early work. Imagine, for instance, a version of *Remain In Light* powered by Ornette Coleman's saxophone rather than Adrian Belew's guitar.

That was not to be, of course. Instead, as the horns joyously shout the melody, Byrne sings of two loves that are like little birds that 'go tweet, tweet, tweet, tweet, tweet, tweet, tweet, tweet'. The verse and chorus are repeated once more, and while this foreshadowing of the big band that would take the stage for *Stop Making Sense* sounds great, the song also feels like a one-off: a track that's not quite true-blue Talking Heads.

115

'I Wish You Wouldn't Say That' (1977) (Byrne)

The B-side to the 'Uh-Oh Love Comes To Town' single features Harrison on guitar and keyboards. Compared to 'Sugar On My Tongue' and 'I Want To Live', the four-person Talking Heads sounds more like a real band and less like three talented kids recording songs in their garage. Harrison plays the hook and adds vibraphone-like fills during the slower parts of this mostly two-chord song.

Like the music, the lyric is less inventive than the songs on *Talking Heads: 77*. The singer is addressing someone who says something he doesn't like, though we never know exactly what that thing is. 'I guess I'll have to make it clearer', he says ironically since not much is clear in this song besides the fact that 'Jimmy's coming over'. Indeed, if any song in Talking Heads' oeuvre sounds borrowed from their CBGB pals the Ramones, it's this one. The song is fun, yes, but also forgettable.

'I Feel It In My Heart' (1977) (Byrne)

The three-person version of Talking Heads play this song in the video *Live At The Kitchen '76*. Byrne strums a white Stratocaster and sings into the mic with his cracked tooth, wearing a green polo shirt with a white collar. Weymouth's eyes are fixed on the back of the singer's head, following his every move, while Frantz nonchalantly plays a vibraphone. The three look like a new band that has practiced a lot (which they had) for their very first (not quite) gig.

The recorded version eschews the vibraphone, but Weymouth's busy bass-playing and Harrison's second guitar more than makeup for the loss. Frantz's drumming is steady, and Byrne shows why he's considered one of the great rock rhythm guitarists. It's a peppy song, which initially appears to be about two lovers who may have to begin their affair again after some unspecified snafu, though the singer wonders, 'What will be the point in being a fool, fool like them?' In verse two, Byrne says he's 'made a decision, revised it again/I saw what it meant to both my parents and friends'. Of course, family and/or friends frequently appear in the first two albums' lyrics (perhaps most strikingly in 'Don't Worry About The Government'), but here you can almost hear Brian Wilson's 'That's Not Me': 'My folks when I wrote them/Told them what I was up to/Said that's not me'. Byrne echoes Wilson's song with eight statements of 'That's not my way'.

As the song builds to its climax, Byrne becomes more and more agitated in stating that this is not his way, he couldn't do it, he couldn't try. Whatever emotional connection was suggested in the song's opening moments is refuted with increasing condemnation. And then, just when Byrne seems on the verge of completely losing it, the opening passage returns and the shouting moves back to real singing. Interestingly, he adds 'If' to the title, giving the nonsense syllables at the end a Byrnian note of ambivalence.

'Sax And Violins' (1991) (Lyrics: Byrne; Music: Byrne, Frantz, Harrison, Weymouth)

'Sax And Violins' begins with solo synthesizer, brooding and heavy on the tremolo. Horror movie-type sounds are introduced, and the track kicks into gear. Most of the music was recorded during the *Naked* sessions, with the core band joined by Wally Badarou on keyboards, Brice Wassy on percussion and cowbell, and Nina Gioia on timbales.

With a mellow groove established, Byrne goes into crooner mode. Appropriate to its corny pun on sex and violence, 'Sax And Violins' introduces elements of jeopardy in its first half. While it's a warm afternoon, the singer asks his love to 'please hold me' as 'It's a dangerous life'. In verse two, the singer says, 'Daddy dear, let's get outta here, I'm scared/Ten o'clock, nighttime in New York, it's weird'. In short, 'If you're looking for trouble/Well, that's where you will find it'. But the next verse shows that the menace is only comic: 'Mom and Pop/They will fuck you up, for sure': How far the Byrnian protagonist has come in his relationship with his parents (not to mention his use of profanity). And, of course, this line alludes to the famous opening of Philip Larkin's poem 'This Be The Verse': 'They fuck you up, your Mum and Dad/They may not mean to, but they do'. On 'Sax And Violins' (which ended the extended 2005 version of *Naked*), the mother and father are potential violent killers, while way back in 1977, on 'Pulled Up' (the final song on the first album), Byrne whooped, 'Mommy, Daddy, come and look at me now/I'm a big man in a great big town!'

After all this menace, the chorus comes as something of a surprise. D has been the dominant chord throughout, and then suddenly, we have D/G/A, with the relative minor thrown in to give the riff a bit of poignancy. The lyric now feels like it could have come from a top 40 song: 'We are criminals who never broke no laws/And all we needed was a net to break our fall'.

After a reprise of the opening, Byrne offers listeners a *mélange* of images: 'searching for diamonds', 'grabbing at straws', 'wooden heads, furniture with legs'. Then, when the chorus returns with its soaring affirmation of love, the background vocals push hard against the uplifting sentiment. 'Shove them, there they are' is sung 46 times, partly with ever-more romantic lines ('Going home where I belong'), but mostly while Byrne is simply humming 'Mm mm mm'. It's a classic Talking Heads surprise attack: the catchy, toe-tapping music is undermined by the cynical lyric.

'Sax And Violins' was included on the soundtrack of the 1991 Wim Wenders science-fiction film *Until The End Of The World*. In the liner notes for *Once In A Lifetime*, Byrne said that when he wrote the lyric in 1990, he tried to imagine the world in 2000, when the movie was set. Among the angles he considered were 'Post-rock sludge with lyrics sponsored by Coke and Pepsi', 'Music created by machines with human shouts of agony and betrayal thrown in', and 'faux Appalachian ballads, the anti-tech wave'. But what he ended up doing was simply composing another classic Talking Heads track.

Alas, despite its popularity with Talking Heads fans, and though this was the band's penultimate single, it made no impression on the *Billboard* Hot 100 or the UK singles chart.

'Gangster Of Love' (1991) (Lyrics: Byrne; Music: Byrne, Frantz, Harrison, Weymouth)

Incorporating music generated for both *Remain In Light* and *Naked*, 'Gangster Of Love' has a slinky feel, with Byrne taking on the role of white funkmeister. The song is addressed to the title character, and the singer spends most of his time berating this person, who drinks cocktails, has a red Mercedes-Benz and seems to think he's the reincarnation of Al Capone. In fact, despite the cool way Byrne sings the song, he seems to be genuinely angry at the gangster, threatening to take him for a ride and hit him right between the eyes before he shoots him down. 'Better hope and pray', the singer concludes, because 'They'll be tearing you apart'.

The keyboard-driven accompaniment is unremarkable, but backing vocalists Arlene Newsome, Phoebe Holmes and Tawatha Agee at times sound like a gospel choir, lending the music a much-needed human touch.

The title might allude to a 1955 blues song of the same name by Johnny 'Guitar' Watson, which includes the line 'I roped 55 girls, and kissed them all at the same time'.

However, Frantz has suggested on several occasions that Byrne might have been jealous of Tom Tom Club's success when he came up with the title. Their biggest US hit was 'Genius Of Love'.

'Lifetime Piling Up' (1992) (Lyrics: Byrne; Music: Byrne, Frantz, Harrison, Weymouth)

Byrne's long practice of putting lyrics to pre-recorded music paid off handsomely in this, one of Talking Heads' strongest songs. However, their final single (released in 1992 after their breakup) did not crack the US Hot 100, though it *did* hit 50 in the UK.

In the liner notes for *Once In A Lifetime*, Jerry Harrison describes this song as one of producer Steve Lillywhite's favorites, and it's easy to see why. The opening lines are vintage Byrne, hearkening back to the comically paranoid lyrics of the band's first years: 'I have tried marijuana/I get nervous every time/They will come a-knockin' at the door'. However, after the humor of the opening verse, the chorus is constructed on a more serious metaphor. Byrne envisions his days turning into nights and the passage of time becoming like the floors of a skyscraper:

Piling them higher, higher, higher
I can feel them swaying back and forth
Building it higher, higher
This tower's leaning over

Brice Wassy is busy on percussion, with Moussa Cissokao joining him on congas. Harrison and Byrne play synthesizers, and again, Tawatha Agee's big backing vocals add depth to Byrne's lead vocal. As on 'Gangster Of Love', Byrne is in no mood to suffer fools: 'Scumbags and superstars, tell me your names/I'll make a bet you're both the same'.

The verse, pre-chorus and chorus use the same two chords, so when the bridge adds three new chords, it sounds like a real change. Each line in the bridge receives an echoing response: 'Cry, cry, cry (Cry, cry, cry)/It's just you and I (It's just you and I)'. The chorus words shift each time it reappears, and by the song's end, the singer's 'lifetime piling up' is 'smashing' into someone else's lifetime. It sounds disastrous, but the song ends on a note that – ironic or not – opens up the possibility of hope. The singer is 'Building that highway to the stars', and the last line is 'Hey, I got a winning number'.

'Popsicle' (1992) (Lyrics: Byrne; Music: Byrne, Frantz, Harrison, Weymouth)
The music for 'Popsicle' was recorded during the *Speaking In Tongues* sessions, and though the lyric was written long after the sessions were over, it very much sounds like a song that just missed the cut. The last track on *Popular Favorites 1976-1992: Sand In The Vaseline*, 'Popsicle' begins with a thumping bass, while Harrison plays simple but funky lines on clavinet and synthesizer. Guitarist Alex Weir and percussionist Steve Scales keep time with Frantz's drumming, which is simple yet designed to support the dancers out on the floor.

The lyric is one of Byrne's most sexual, with the barely concealed double-entendres:

Mmm, something sweet and sticky
Mmm, running down my hand
Popsicle of love

He's even more forthright in verse two, where we hear about 'a kinky little sister ... wearing rubber gloves' who is there in a 'sexual health emergency'. Talking Heads were always big fans of James Brown, and 'Popsicle' feels like something of a tribute to the raw id found in so many songs by the Godfather of Soul.

Once the song's conceit is established, there are not really any surprises other than a few sexual jokes (and a nod to Cab Calloway): 'Hit me in my funny bone/Hi-De-Ho, tootsie roll/Jelly roll, it's time to go'. Thankfully, Tawatha Agee's powerful vocal keeps the song lively and makes its sometimes-sophomoric lyric sound like it has some weight.

Ultimately, 'Popsicle' is a song that aims to be *fun*, and it certainly achieves that end. Byrne's singing is jubilant, and he plays some mean licks on the MiniMoog. Granted, at 5:20 in length, the song with its long fade-out on the throwaway lines 'Summertime, summertime, ooh' and 'Sugar bee, sugar bee, ooh' is probably too long, but that's okay. After all, as Byrne sings in an insinuating voice, 'It's summertime, Boy'.

'In Asking Land' (2003) (Lyrics: Byrne; Music: Byrne, Frantz, Harrison, Weymouth)
The only previously unreleased song on *Once In A Lifetime: The Talking Head Box* (55 songs and 233 minutes of music) was the four-minute track 'In Asking Land'. An outtake from *Naked*, it had previously been reworked into 'Carnival Eyes' on Byrne's solo album *Rei Momo* after the *de facto* end of Talking Heads. 'Carnival Eyes' gives the song a Latin flavor and presents us with a character named Carnival Girl as the song's protagonist: a young lady who lives in an uncertain world of soldiers and praying women.

Carnival Girl is absent from 'In Asking Land', but many of the words are the same. While there is relatively little information about the track's recording, it begins with guitar and percussion, quiet and a touch menacing. When Byrne begins singing, the acoustic ensemble rises in volume and energy to support his narrative. The singer launches into an elliptical story that seems to be told from the point of view of someone quite different from himself. The narrator – possibly a woman – tells us that 'someone else's son' has 'gone away'. Every night, the speaker lies there with a 'hard hurt heart' while someone 'Buried in time/Lay in the factory bleeding'.

'All the time they walk the line', the singer tells us, 'And all the time in asking land'. Later, the lines 'All the miners breathing underground' and 'Down they go/Why are we left behind?' suggest the possibility that the song is in response to the 1984/1985 United Kingdom miners' strike, where the miners, whose work was normally down inside the earth, walked picket lines instead. We know that most of Byrne's work with Talking Heads was not directly political, but the miners' strike was an international story, replete with arrests, pit closures, job losses, injuries, and six deaths.

Towards the end, the speaker imagines being 'like a wet, cold miner', picturing the face of the person who has been lost in the grasses that grow through rock and stone. The final verse asks, 'What does it mean?/Is there no golden law?' In any event, 'Now that he's done/It's not the same'.

Of course, Byrne never makes things easy for interpreters of his lyrics, but the couplet in the song's center – 'What is a man?/What are we working for?' – raises questions that the miners continually asked themselves and their employers. Whatever the specifics refer to, the song is one that argues for human dignity in the face of a cold, uncaring adversary.

Talking Heads ... *On Track*

Epilogue

The three-member version of Talking Heads played their first gig at CBGB in May 1975. In December 1991, three years after their final album, Byrne mentioned casually in a *Los Angeles Times* interview that the band had 'broken up, or call it whatever you like'. *Naked*, released in 1988, was essentially their final outing together, but 13 years is a long run for any successful rock band. Ideally, everyone should have ended the partnership proud of their success and happy to move on to new projects and adventures. Unfortunately, interpersonal squabbles – particularly between Weymouth and Byrne – have been a part of the band's dynamic almost from the start, and they are ongoing even as this book goes to press.

Writing in *Salon*, David Bowman recounted a 1996 Byrne interview where the singer explained why the band never regrouped:

'I'd get these bizarre letters from Tina', he said, gritting his teeth. 'They'd say what a fucking dumb jerk and asshole piece of shit I was. It would go into detail how badly I'd behaved, what a terrible person I was, how hard I was to work with, how unfair I was. It was this thing meant to make me feel real terrible, and how much 'I hate you, I hate you, I hate you'. And then, in the end, she'd go, 'Why don't you want to work with us? Why in the world don't you want to work with us? What's the matter?' Byrne paused and sighed. 'You've answered the question. Look at the beginning of your letter, look at the end. You've answered it. There is some kind of weird denial going on'.

Or, as Byrne put it in an earlier interview, 'It's like being told, 'You should get back with your first wife. You guys were good together'. Well, I think most people would pass on an offer like that'.

Weymouth's take is very different. It's hard to find an extended interview with her in which she doesn't cast at least a little shade on Byrne. A 2022 interview with *Far Out* magazine is a good example: 'I think everybody was always afraid David would crack or break. You really had to walk on eggs, and he could be a bully, but you couldn't do it to *him*. He could be unfaithful, but you have to be loyal. It's very Trumpian, in a way. One needed sacrifices in order to keep it going because we absolutely adored our fans. David never cared about people. But we did, and we loved our team'.

For all its essential inside information on the making of the band's music, Frantz's *Remain In Love* does feel fairly one-sided. As the book's title indicates, Frantz loves his wife, and he gives the impression that musical and lyrical genius notwithstanding, Byrne is basically a stuck-up jerk. As Jonathan Gould noted in a 2023 *New Yorker* story, Frantz 'rarely misses an opportunity to point out instances of Byrne's awkwardness, obtuseness, aloofness and grandiosity'.

But how much of Byrne's behavior was artistic ego, and how much had to do with his self-admitted autism? When Terry Gross asked Byrne on NPR's

121

Fresh Air why, if he felt he was on the autism spectrum, he'd never been treated, he replied, 'Probably because I thought, this is just me. I'm not unhappy. I might be a little bit different than some other people, but I'm not unhappy. This is the way I experience the world, but I'm doing fine. I really enjoy writing the songs and performing and the other things that we do. So why act like I have something wrong that needs to be treated?'

Looking at Byrne's Wikipedia page – which one assumes he had a hand in curating – one can't help but feel that he considers or wants to consider his time with Talking Heads as simply one episode in a very long artistic career. For hardcore Byrne fans, that assessment may ring true. But for Talking Heads fans, Byrne's side projects and post-band music and media may feel like an unfortunate postscript. What if all that creative energy had been channeled into the band that understood Byrne like perhaps no other group of musicians?

However, in a way, Byrne's decision to break the band up acknowledged the importance of the other band members. In *This Must Be The Place*, he is quoted as saying, 'Our kind of band was the result of camaraderie, and the music emerged out of that – when we were hanging out, we were all in it together. When that stops, you might as well be making music with anybody. Which is what happened, with me anyway'. As Bowman points out, the band hadn't really hung out together since 1980, 'So they'd made a good go of it, all things considering'.

An epilogue is an ending, but it's difficult to compose an epitaph for Talking Heads. As I write, all four members are still alive and well. According to the band's official website bio, Harrison, in addition to producing numerous musical acts and moving to San Francisco in 1994, 'founded four companies: Garageband.com, Ophirex, RedCrow and The Main Stage'. He has also served on the board of directors for MicroUnity Engineering, IODA, iLike and Carbon Gold. Like Brian May of Queen, Harrison is a very smart guy who likely would have succeeded in any field he entered.

In *Remain In Love*, Frantz summarizes the life he and his wife chose after the band broke up: 'We built a great recording studio of our own, and started making and producing records again. We spent more time with our family and friends'. *No Talking Just Head* – an album by Frantz, Weymouth, Harrison and an array of guest vocalists (an ensemble billed as The Heads) – wasn't well received. But Frantz and Weymouth have continued performing with a rotating cast of side musicians, as Tom Tom Club. Frantz writes of spending time in Paris and the French countryside, sailing on their yacht from the Bahamas to Maine, eating, drinking and living well with his wife and their two adult children. It sounds like a pretty good life.

With Byrne's musical *American Utopia,* which was made up of his own and Talking Heads songs, he has finally reached the commercial solo success he sought in the decades since the band broke up. A live recording of the Broadway show was nominated for a Grammy for Best Musical Theater

Album, and Spike Lee's documentary and concert film has received popular and critical acclaim. Byrne even collaborated on a picture book of the show, with illustrations by Maira Kalman.

Perhaps things didn't turn out so badly for the four of them after all.

Moreover, the wildly successful re-release of their film *Stop Making Sense* (the ownership of which is split equally between the four of them) found the former bandmates making a busy round of media interviews, mostly managing to express a fondness for each other and their shared endeavor. Nearly always, they were asked if they would get back together, even being offered $80,000,000 to do a tour that included headlining Coachella. But nothing, it seemed, could tempt them to reunite.

Fortunately, the magic of recorded music means that old and new fans continue to buy, copy, stream, watch and generally consume Talking Heads' magnificent and varied catalog. And for someone just coming to the music, a whole world is about to open up. For those listeners, a few words of advice: it's a lot to handle. Take your time. Don't be afraid. Stop making sense if it helps. Just remember that everyone breathing and everyone dead – all of us – live in a city of dreams.

Also available from Sonicbond

On Track series
AC/DC – Chris Sutton 978-1-78952-307-2
Allman Brothers Band – Andrew Wild 978-1-78952-252-5
Tori Amos – Lisa Torem 978-1-78952-142-9
Aphex Twin – Beau Waddell 978-1-78952-267-9
Asia – Peter Braidis 978-1-78952-099-6
Badfinger – Robert Day-Webb 978-1-878952-176-4
Barclay James Harvest – Keith and Monica Domone 978-1-78952-067-5
Beck – Arthur Lizie 978-1-78952-258-7
The Beat, General Public, Fine Young Cannibals – Steve Parry 978-1-78952-274-7
The Beatles 1962-1996 – Alberto Bravin and Andrew Wild 978-1-78952-355-3
The Beatles Solo 1969-1980 – Andrew Wild 978-1-78952-030-9
Blue Oyster Cult – Jacob Holm-Lupo 978-1-78952-007-1
Blur – Matt Bishop 978-178952-164-1
Marc Bolan and T.Rex – Peter Gallagher 978-1-78952-124-5
David Bowie 1964 to 1982 – Carl Ewens 978-1-78952-324-9
David Bowie 1963 to 2016 – Don Klees 978-1-78952-351-5
Kate Bush – Bill Thomas 978-1-78952-097-2
The Byrds – Andy McArthur 978-1-78952-280-8
Camel – Hamish Kuzminski 978-1-78952-040-8
Captain Beefheart – Opher Goodwin 978-1-78952-235-8
Caravan – Andy Boot 978-1-78952-127-6
Cardiacs – Eric Benac 978-1-78952-131-3
Wendy Carlos – Mark Marrington 978-1-78952-331-7
The Carpenters – Paul Tornbohm 978-1-78952-301-0
Nick Cave and The Bad Seeds – Dominic Sanderson 978-1-78952-240-2
Eric Clapton Solo – Andrew Wild 978-1-78952-141-2
The Clash (revised edition) – Nick Assirati 978-1-78952-325-6
Elvis Costello and The Attractions – Georg Purvis 978-1-78952-129-0
Crosby, Stills and Nash – Andrew Wild 978-1-78952-039-2
Creedence Clearwater Revival – Tony Thompson 978-1-78952-237-2
Crowded House – Jon Magidsohn 978-1-78952-292-1
The Damned – Morgan Brown 978-1-78952-136-8
David Bowie 1964 to 1982 – Carl Ewens 978-1-78952-324-9
David Bowie 1964 to 1982 – Carl Ewens 978-1-78952-324-9
Deep Purple and Rainbow 1968-79 – Steve Pilkington 978-1-78952-002-6
Deep Purple from 1984 – Phil Kafcaloudes 978-1-78952-354-6
Depeche Mode – Brian J. Robb 978-1-78952-277-8
Dire Straits – Andrew Wild 978-1-78952-044-6
The Divine Comedy – Alan Draper 978-1-78952-308-9
The Doors – Tony Thompson 978-1-78952-137-5
Dream Theater – Jordan Blum 978-1-78952-050-7
Bob Dylan 1962-1970 – Opher Goodwin 978-1-78952-275-2
Eagles – John Van der Kiste 978-1-78952-260-0
Earth, Wind and Fire – Bud Wilkins 978-1-78952-272-3
Electric Light Orchestra – Barry Delve 978-1-78952-152-8
Emerson Lake and Palmer – Mike Goode 978-1-78952-000-2
Fairport Convention – Kevan Furbank 978-1-78952-051-4
Peter Gabriel – Graeme Scarfe 978-1-78952-138-2
Genesis – Stuart MacFarlane 978-1-78952-005-7
Gentle Giant – Gary Steel 978-1-78952-058-3
Gong – Kevan Furbank 978-1-78952-082-8
Green Day – William E. Spevack 978-1-78952-261-7
Steve Hackett – Geoffrey Feakes 978-1-78952-098-9
Hall and Oates – Ian Abrahams 978-1-78952-167-2
Peter Hammill – Richard Rees Jones 978-1-78952-163-4
Roy Harper – Opher Goodwin 978-1-78952-130-6
Hawkwind (new edition) – Duncan Harris 978-1-78952-290-7
Jimi Hendrix – Emma Stott 978-1-78952-175-7

Also available from Sonicbond

The Hollies – Andrew Darlington 978-1-78952-159-7
Horslips – Richard James 978-1-78952-263-1
The Human League and The Sheffield Scene – Andrew Darlington 978-1-78952-186-3
Humble Pie –Robert Day-Webb 978-1-78952-2761
Ian Hunter – G. Mick Smith 978-1-78952-304-1
The Incredible String Band – Tim Moon 978-1-78952-107-8
INXS – Manny Grillo 978-1-78952-302-7
Iron Maiden – Steve Pilkington 978-1-78952-061-3
Joe Jackson – Richard James 978-1-78952-189-4
The Jam – Stan Jeffries 978-1-78952-299-0
Jefferson Airplane – Richard Butterworth 978-1-78952-143-6
Jethro Tull – Jordan Blum 978-1-78952-016-3
J. Geils Band – James Romag 978-1-78952-332-4
Elton John in the 1970s – Peter Kearns 978-1-78952-034-7
Billy Joel – Lisa Torem 978-1-78952-183-2
Journey – Doug Thornton 978-1-78952-337-9
Judas Priest – John Tucker 978-1-78952-018-7
Kansas – Kevin Cummings 978-1-78952-057-6
Killing Joke – Nic Ransome 978-1-78952-273-0
The Kinks – Martin Hutchinson 978-1-78952-172-6
Korn – Matt Karpe 978-1-78952-153-5
Led Zeppelin – Steve Pilkington 978-1-78952-151-1
Level 42 – Matt Philips 978-1-78952-102-3
Little Feat – Georg Purvis – 978-1-78952-168-9
Magnum – Matthew Taylor – 978-1-78952-286-0
Aimee Mann – Jez Rowden 978-1-78952-036-1
Ralph McTell – Paul O. Jenkins 978-1-78952-294-5
Metallica – Barry Wood 978-1-78952-269-3
Joni Mitchell – Peter Kearns 978-1-78952-081-1
The Moody Blues – Geoffrey Feakes 978-1-78952-042-2
Motorhead – Duncan Harris 978-1-78952-173-3
Nektar – Scott Meze – 978-1-78952-257-0
New Order – Dennis Remmer – 978-1-78952-249-5
Nightwish – Simon McMurdo – 978-1-78952-270-9
Nirvana – William E. Spevack 978-1-78952-318-8
Laura Nyro – Philip Ward 978-1-78952-182-5
Oasis – Andrew Rooney 978-1-78952-300-3
Phil Ochs – Opher Goodwin 978-1-78952-326-3
Mike Oldfield – Ryan Yard 978-1-78952-060-6
Opeth – Jordan Blum 978-1-78-952-166-5
Pearl Jam – Ben L. Connor 978-1-78952-188-7
Tom Petty – Richard James 978-1-78952-128-3
Pink Floyd – Richard Butterworth 978-1-78952-242-6
The Police – Pete Braidis 978-1-78952-158-0
Porcupine Tree (Revised Edition) – Nick Holmes 978-1-78952-346-1
Procol Harum – Scott Meze 978-1-78952-315-7
Queen – Andrew Wild 978-1-78952-003-3
Radiohead – William Allen 978-1-78952-149-8
Gerry Rafferty – John Van der Kiste 978-1-78952-349-2
Rancid – Paul Matts 978-1-78952-187-0
Lou Reed 1972-1986 – Ethan Roy 978-1-78952-283-9
Renaissance – David Detmer 978-1-78952-062-0
REO Speedwagon – Jim Romag 978-1-78952-262-4
The Rolling Stones 1963-80 – Steve Pilkington 978-1-78952-017-0
Linda Ronstadt 1969-1989 – Daryl O. Lawrence 987-1-78952-293-8
Roxy Music – Michael Kulikowski 978-1-78952-335-5
Rush 1973 to 1982 – Richard James 978-1-78952-338-6
Sensational Alex Harvey Band – Peter Gallagher 978-1-7952-289-1
The Small Faces and The Faces – Andrew Darlington 978-1-78952-316-4

Also available from Sonicbond

The Smashing Pumpkins – Matt Karpe 978-1-7952-291-4
The Smiths and Morrissey – Tommy Gunnarsson 978-1-78952-140-5
Soft Machine – Scott Meze 978-1078952-271-6
Sparks 1969-1979 – Chris Sutton 978-1-78952-279-2
Spirit – Rev. Keith A. Gordon – 978-1-78952- 248-8
Stackridge – Alan Draper 978-1-78952-232-7
Status Quo the Frantic Four Years – Richard James 978-1-78952-160-3
Steely Dan – Jez Rowden 978-1-78952-043-9
The Stranglers – Martin Hutchinson 978-1-78952-323-2
Talk Talk – Gary Steel 978-1-78952-284-6
Talking Heads – David Starkey 978-178952-353-9
Tears For Fears – Paul Clark – 978-178952-238-9
Thin Lizzy – Graeme Stroud 978-1-78952-064-4
Tool – Matt Karpe 978-1-78952-234-1
Toto – Jacob Holm-Lupo 978-1-78952-019-4
U2 – Eoghan Lyng 978-1-78952-078-1
UFO – Richard James 978-1-78952-073-6
Ultravox – Brian J. Robb 978-1-78952-330-0
Van Der Graaf Generator – Dan Coffey 978-1-78952-031-6
Van Halen – Morgan Brown – 9781-78952-256-3
Suzanne Vega – Lisa Torem 978-1-78952-281-5
Jack White And The White Stripes – Ben L. Connor 978-1-78952-303-4
The Who – Geoffrey Feakes 978-1-78952-076-7
Roy Wood and the Move – James R Turner 978-1-78952-008-8
Yes (new edition) – Stephen Lambe 978-1-78952-282-2
Neil Young 1963 to 1970 – Oper Goodwin 978-1-78952-298-3
Frank Zappa 1966 to 1979 – Eric Benac 978-1-78952-033-0
Warren Zevon – Peter Gallagher 978-1-78952-170-2
The Zombies – Emma Stott 978-1-78952-297-6
10CC – Peter Kearns 978-1-78952-054-5

Decades Series
The Bee Gees in the 1960s – Andrew Mon Hughes et al 978-1-78952-148-1
The Bee Gees in the 1970s – Andrew Mon Hughes et al 978-1-78952-179-5
Black Sabbath in the 1970s – Chris Sutton 978-1-78952-171-9
Britpop – Peter Richard Adams and Matt Pooler 978-1-78952-169-6
Phil Collins in the 1980s – Andrew Wild 978-1-78952-185-6
Alice Cooper in the 1970s – Chris Sutton 978-1-78952-104-7
Alice Cooper in the 1980s – Chris Sutton 978-1-78952-259-4
Curved Air in the 1970s – Laura Shenton 978-1-78952-069-9
Donovan in the 1960s – Jeff Fitzgerald 978-1-78952-233-4
Bob Dylan in the 1980s – Don Klees 978-1-78952-157-3
Brian Eno in the 1970s – Gary Parsons 978-1-78952-239-6
Faith No More in the 1990s – Matt Karpe 978-1-78952-250-1
Fleetwood Mac in the 1970s – Andrew Wild 978-1-78952-105-4
Fleetwood Mac in the 1980s – Don Klees 978-178952-254-9
Focus in the 1970s – Stephen Lambe 978-1-78952-079-8
Free and Bad Company in the 1970s – John Van der Kiste 978-1-78952-178-8
Genesis in the 1970s – Bill Thomas 978178952-146-7
George Harrison in the 1970s – Eoghan Lyng 978-1-78952-174-0
Kiss in the 1970s – Peter Gallagher 978-1-78952-246-4
Manfred Mann's Earth Band in the 1970s – John Van der Kiste 978178952-243-3
Marillion in the 1980s – Nathaniel Webb 978-1-78952-065-1
Van Morrison in the 1970s – Peter Childs – 978-1-78952-241-9
Mott the Hoople & Ian Hunter in the 1970s – John Van der Kiste 978-1-78-952-162-7
Pink Floyd In The 1970s – Georg Purvis 978-1-78952-072-9
Suzi Quatro in the 1970s – Darren Johnson 978-1-78952-236-5
Queen in the 1970s – James Griffiths 978-1-78952-265-5
Roxy Music in the 1970s – Dave Thompson 978-1-78952-180-1

Also available from Sonicbond

Slade in the 1970s – Darren Johnson 978-1-78952-268-6
Status Quo in the 1980s – Greg Harper 978-1-78952-244-0
Tangerine Dream in the 1970s – Stephen Palmer 978-1-78952-161-0
The Sweet in the 1970s – Darren Johnson 978-1-78952-139-9
Uriah Heep in the 1970s – Steve Pilkington 978-1-78952-103-0
Van der Graaf Generator in the 1970s – Steve Pilkington 978-1-78952-245-7
Rick Wakeman in the 1970s – Geoffrey Feakes 978-1-78952-264-8
Yes in the 1980s – Stephen Lambe with David Watkinson 978-1-78952-125-2

Rock Classics Series
90125 by Yes – Stephen Lambe 978-1-78952-329-4
Bat Out Of Hell by Meatloaf – Geoffrey Feakes 978-1-78952-320-1
Bringing It All Back Home by Bob Dylan – Opher Goodwin 978-1-78952-314-0
Californication by Red Hot Chili Peppers - Matt Karpe 978-1-78952-348-5
Crime Of The Century by Supertramp – Steve Pilkington 978-1-78952-327-0
The Dreaming by Kate Bush – Peter Kearns 978-1-78952-341-6
Let It Bleed by The Rolling Stones – John Van der Kiste 978-1-78952-309-6
Pawn Hearts by Van Der Graaf Generator – Paolo Carnelli 978-1-78952-357-7
Purple Rain by Prince – Matt Karpe 978-1-78952-322-5
The White Album by The Beatles – Opher Goodwin 978-1-78952-333-1

On Screen Series
Carry On... – Stephen Lambe 978-1-78952-004-0
David Cronenberg – Patrick Chapman 978-1-78952-071-2
Doctor Who: The David Tennant Years – Jamie Hailstone 978-1-78952-066-8
James Bond – Andrew Wild 978-1-78952-010-1
Monty Python – Steve Pilkington 978-1-78952-047-7
Seinfeld Seasons 1 to 5 – Stephen Lambe 978-1-78952-012-5

Other Books
1967: A Year In Psychedelic Rock 978-1-78952-155-9
1970: A Year In Rock – John Van der Kiste 978-1-78952-147-4
1972: The Year Progressive Rock Ruled The World – Kevan Furbank 978-1-78952-288-4
1973: The Golden Year of Progressive Rock 978-1-78952-165-8
Eric Clapton Sessions – Andrew Wild 978-1-78952-177-1
Dark Horse Records – Aaron Badgley 978-1-78952-287-7
Derek Taylor: For Your Radioactive Children – Andrew Darlington 978-1-78952-038-5
Ghosts – Journeys To Post-Pop – Matthew Restall 978-1-78952-334-8
The Golden Age of Easy Listening – Derek Taylor 978-1-78952-285-3
The Golden Road: The Recording History of The Grateful Dead – John Kilbride 978-1-78952-156-6
Hoggin' The Page – Groudhogs The Classic Years – Martyn Hanson 978-1-78952-343-0
Iggy and The Stooges On Stage 1967-1974 – Per Nilsen 978-1-78952-101-6
Jon Anderson and the Warriors – the Road to Yes – David Watkinson 978-1-78952-059-0
Magic: The David Paton Story – David Paton 978-1-78952-266-2
Misty: The Music of Johnny Mathis – Jakob Baekgaard 978-1-78952-247-1
Musical Guide To Red By King Crimson – Andrew Keeling 978-1-78952-321-8
Nu Metal: A Definitive Guide – Matt Karpe 978-1-78952-063-7
Philip Lynott – Renegade – Alan Byrne 978-1-78952-339-3
Remembering Live Aid – Andrew Wild 978-1-78952-328-7
Thank You For The Days - Fans Of The Kinks Share 60 Years of Stories – Ed. Chris Kocher 978-1-78952-342-3
The Sonicbond On Track Sampler – 978-1-78952-190-0
The Sonicbond Progressive Rock Sampler (Ebook only) – 978-1-78952-056-9
Tommy Bolin: In and Out of Deep Purple – Laura Shenton 978-1-78952-070-5
Maximum Darkness – Deke Leonard 978-1-78952-048-4
The Twang Dynasty – Deke Leonard 978-1-78952-049-1

... and many more to come!

Would you like to write for Sonicbond Publishing?

At Sonicbond Publishing we are always on the look-out for authors, particularly for our two main series:

On Track. Mixing fact with in depth analysis, the On Track series examines the work of a particular musical artist or group. All genres are considered from easy listening and jazz to 60s soul to 90s pop, via rock and metal.

On Screen. This series looks at the world of film and television. Subjects considered include directors, actors and writers, as well as entire television and film series. As with the On Track series, we balance fact with analysis.

While professional writing experience would, of course, be an advantage the most important qualification is to have real enthusiasm and knowledge of your subject. First-time authors are welcomed, but the ability to write well in English is essential.

Sonicbond Publishing has distribution throughout Europe and North America, and all books are also published in E-book form. Authors will be paid a royalty based on sales of their book.

Further details are available from www.sonicbondpublishing.co.uk. To contact us, complete the contact form there or email info@sonicbondpublishing.co.uk